SHE CAME IN THROUGH THE KITCHEN WINDOW

Recipes Inspired by the Beatles and Their Music

Stephen J. Spignesi

CITADEL PRESS
Kensington Publishing Corp.
www.kensingtonbooks.com

CITADEL PRESS BOOKS are published by

Kensington Publishing Corp.
850 Third Avenue
New York, NY 10022

First hardcover edition: 2000

All Kensington titles, imprints, and distributed lines are
available at special quantity discounts for bulk purchases for
sales promotions, premiums, fund-raising, edicational, or
institutional use. Special book excerpts or customized printings
can also be created to fit specific needs. For details, write or
phone the office of the Kensington special sales manager:
Kensington Publishing Corp., 850 Third Avenue, New York, NY
10022, attn: Special Sales Department, phone 1-800-221-2647.

First Trade Paperback printing: June 2002
10   9   8   7   6   5   4   3   2   1

Printed in the United States of America

Cataloging data may be obtained from the Library of Congress

ISBN 0-8065-2359-X

To two remarkable Mikes—
Streeto and Lewis:

*I'd like to say thank you
on behalf of the group and ourselves*

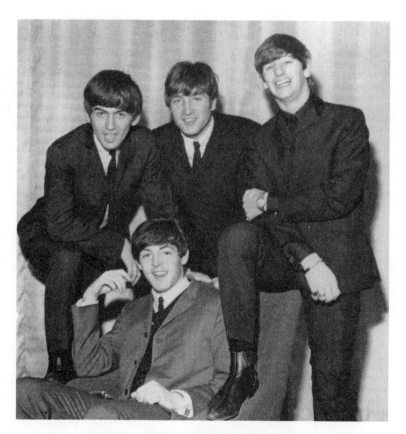

Relaxing after a satisfying Beatles feast.
(Photo courtesy of Photofest)

Contents

Acknowledgments

First and foremost I'd again like to thank my Beatles Support Team, the inestimable trio of Tom Schultheiss, Mike Lewis, and Dan Fasano. These guys really *know* the Beatles, and their wide-ranging knowledge has enhanced much of what I have written about the Beatles, both in this book and in my previous book about the Fabs, *The Beatles Book of Lists.* Dan Fasano, in particular, contributed in several ways to yet *another* Beatles book I am working on, and I greatly appreciate his input and suggestions.

I'd also like to single out the super-groovy, always fab, Mike "Ringo" Streeto, and thank him for his help, his friendship, and his support. Mike has an awesome mental repository of not only Beatles facts and figures but also all manner of pop-culture info, and he has always shared his wealth of knowledge with me in any way he could in order to help me with my research. Mike is also a musician and a writer and will undoubtedly turn his attention to writing his own book one day. That's a book I will be waiting in line to read. Thanks, Mike.

I'd also like to thank my agent John White, who knows why.

Charlie Fried is another good friend who deserves a nod and my thanks.

Several people contributed fabulous recipes to this book, including Pam Spignesi, Lee Mandato, Erik Leeming, Mary and Ray Pantalena,

Rosalie Merola, Mike Lewis, Dolores Fantarella, George Beahm, Cheryl Tucker, and many others. My gratitude to them all.

Also, my thanks to Steven Schragis, Bruce Bender, Susan Hayes, Lynda Dickey, Renata Butera, Karen Quinn, and all the other fine folks at Carol Publishing.

Clutching Forks and Knives!

. . . had a laugh and over dinner . . .

The Beatles are more than a musical group. Let's face it . . . the Beatles are a bloomin' *lifestyle!*

She Came In Through the Kitchen Window: Recipes Inspired by the Beatles and Their Music presents dozens of delicious recipes for your gustatory enjoyment, every one of which was inspired by a Beatle or a Beatles song.

May I suggest that you use this cookbook to create several different Beatles menus, choosing different appetizers, breads, salads, sauces, entrées, beverages, and desserts from the book, and have a Beatles Feast as often as possible.

The background music must be (of course) the Dave Clark Five!

Sorry . . . just kidding.

Programmable CD players are a blessing for Beatles fans. It is now possible to have an endless stream of Beatles music playing in your home, and your in-house Fab Four performance can consist of, for instance, nothing but the complete *Beatles Anthology;* or a chronological delight made up of *Please Please Me, With The Beatles!, A Hard Day's Night, Help!,* and *Rubber Soul.* (Wow. What a listening party, eh?)

For those truly special dinner parties, there's no debate: It's got to be *Sgt. Pepper,* the *White Album,* and *Abbey Road,* in that order, with no breaks between.

The recipes in *She Came In Through the Kitchen Window* are wide ranging, delicious, and, for the most part, not too difficult to prepare. All the ingredients should be available at any good supermarket, and the equipment you'll need is (I'd bet on it) already in your kitchen cabinets. Read the entire recipe first before you begin, so you'll be better prepared once you get started.

A word of caution, though. If, while reading this book and preparing these delicious dishes, you find yourself humming, whistling, or—worst yet—singing your *own* versions of "food-inspired" Beatles tunes, we assume no responsibility for the consequences.

Beatles appétit!

IMPORTANT NOTE: Unless otherwise indicated, all milk is whole milk; all mozzarella is whole-milk mozzarella; and all oregano, cinnamon, and parsley are ground. The choice of brown sugar (light or dark), unless specifically denoted, is up to the individual cook. For recipes that call for lemon juice, it is the cook's option to use either the juice squeezed from a fresh lemon or bottled lemon juice.

The Food Four: Twenty-seven Beatles Songs With Eating or Food References

Here is a rundown of the twenty-seven Beatles songs in which food or eating is mentioned. Following the title is the lyrical gastronomic reference.

"The Ballad of John and Yoko"
(acorns, chocolate cake, eating)
"Come Together" (Coca-Cola)
"Cry Baby Cry" (breakfast, kitchen)
"Doctor Robert" (drink)
"Drive My Car" (peanuts)
"Get Back" [LP] (frying pan)
"Glass Onion" (onion)
"Her Majesty" (wine)
"I Am the Walrus" (cornflakes, custard, semolina)
"I Don't Want to Spoil the Party" (drink)
"I Me Mine" (wine)
"I'm So Tired" (drink)
"It's All Too Much" (cake)
"Lovely Rita" (dinner)
"Lucy in the Sky With Diamonds" (eat, marmalade, marshmallow pies)
"Mean Mr. Mustard" (mustard)
"Norwegian Wood (This Bird Has Flown)" (drinking, wine)
"Penny Lane" (fish and finger pie)
"Piggies" (bacon, dinner, eat, forks)
"Rain" (lemonade)

"Rocky Raccoon" (gin)
"Savoy Truffle" (apple tart, coconut fudge, coffee dessert, cherry cream, crème tangerine, eat, ginger sling with a pineapple heart)
"She Came In Through the Bathroom Window" (silver spoon)
"She's Leaving Home" (kitchen)
"Strawberry Fields Forever" (cranberry sauce, strawberry)
"Sun King" (cake, eat)
"When I'm Sixty-Four" (wine)

All four Beatles also released solo songs pertaining to food, cooking, or eating:

John: "Cold Turkey," "Meat City," "Beef Jerky"
Paul: "Eat at Home," "Lunch Box/Odd Sox," "Cook of the House," "Soggy Noodle"
George: "Thanks for the Pepperoni"
Ringo: "Cookin' in the Kitchen of Love," "Brandy"

"Good Morning, Good Morning" Breakfasts and Brunches

All Things Must Pass Bran Muffins

("All Things Must Pass")

George was singing about earthly hardships when he wrote his classic, "All Things Must Pass," so please forgive the sacreligious double entendre in the name of these wonderful (and, ahem, "stimulating") bran muffins. (This 1970 solo Harrison effort technically became a Beatles song in 1996 when it appeared on *Anthology 3.*)

INGREDIENTS
  2 cups (550 ml) 100% bran
    cereal
  1 cup (235 ml) boiling water
  ¼ cup (70 ml) sugar
  ½ cup (140 ml) shortening
  2 medium eggs
  2 cups (475 ml) buttermilk
2½ cups (690 ml) all-purpose
    flour
2½ teaspoons baking soda

  ¾ teaspoon salt
  1 teaspoon cinnamon
  1 teaspoon finely shredded
    lemon peel
  2 cups (550 ml) All-Bran
    cereal

EQUIPMENT
2 small bowls
1 large bowl
Muffin tin with 48 cups

Preheat the oven to 350° F (177° C). In a small bowl, combine the 100 percent bran cereal and the boiling water. Set this mixture aside to cool.

In a larger bowl, mix together the sugar and the shortening. To this mixture add the eggs, one at a time. Add the buttermilk and cooled bran cereal mixture to this bowl. In another small bowl, mix together the flour, baking soda, salt, cinnamon, and shredded lemon peel, and add to the large bowl. Stir into this the All-Bran cereal.

Grease the muffin cups and fill them each three-quarters full with the muffin batter. Bake for 25 minutes. Makes 48 muffins.

Did you know . . . ?

 George Harrison met his first wife, Pattie Boyd, during the filming of *A Hard Day's Night.* Pattie was hired as an extra and can be seen in the "I Should Have Known Better" scene on the train.

I Am the Scrambled Eggman

("I Am the Walrus")

Were the Rutles thinking of this delicious cheesy-onion scrambled egg omelet when they recorded their Lennonesque song "Cheese and Onions"? Just wondering.

INGREDIENTS
1 medium green onion (or 1
   large green onion, if you're
   an onion lover)
1 tablespoon salted butter
6 medium eggs
⅓ cup (80 ml) milk
¼ teaspoon salt
   Dash black pepper

½ cup (140 ml) shredded
   American cheese

EQUIPMENT
Large skillet
Mixing bowl
Spatula

Slice the green onion and cook it in a skillet in butter for 30 seconds. In a bowl, beat together the eggs, milk, salt, and a dash of black pepper. Add the egg mixture to the green onions in the skillet. When the eggs begin to set, add the shredded American cheese. Finish cooking to your preferred consistency. Serve with toast and jam. (Baby You're a Peach Jam on page 7 goes especially well with this.) Serves 3.

Did you know . . . ?

● Paul's original title for "Yesterday" was "Scrambled Eggs."

Happiness Is a Warm Bun

("Happiness Is a Warm Gun")

These delicious cinnamon rolls would make even a stern-faced Mother Superior smile and sing their praises!

INGREDIENTS
¾ *cup (180 ml) warm milk*
¼ *cup (70 ml) sugar*
 1 *teaspoon salt*
¼ *cup (½ stick) salted butter, softened*
1¼ *tablespoons cinnamon*
 2 *medium eggs*
 1 *package (¼ ounce/18 g) dry yeast*

¼ *cup (60 ml) warm water*
2½ *cups (690 ml) all-purpose flour*

EQUIPMENT
2 large mixing bowls
Large bowl greased with butter
Baking tin

In a large mixing bowl, mix the milk, sugar, salt, butter, cinnamon, and eggs. Let the mixture cool to lukewarm. In another bowl, stir the yeast into the warm water and let stand for 5 minutes, until it is fully dissolved. Pour the dissolved yeast into the first bowl and beat thoroughly. Add 1½ cups (415 ml) of the flour and beat well. Cover the bowl and let the dough rise in a warm place for approximately 1 hour.

Add the remaining flour to the dough and blend well. Add more flour if needed to give the dough a firm consistency. Knead the dough thoroughly until it is smooth and stretchy. Put it in a large buttered bowl, cover, and allow it to rise until it is approximately double in

Happiness is a Warm Bun, especially after a day on and off the skis.
(Photo courtesy of Photofest)

size. Punch the dough down, roll it into a long log 2 to 3 inches (5 to 8 cm) in diameter, and cut it into 18 rolls. Allow the rolls to rise for 1 hour.

While you're waiting, preheat the oven to 450° F (232° C). Bake for 15 to 20 minutes. Serve the buns hot with butter, jelly, or Baby You're a Peach Jam (below). Makes 18 cinnamon rolls.

Did you know . . . ?

🍎 Paul McCartney's favorite song on the Beatles' *White Album* is John's "Happiness Is a Warm Gun."

Baby You're a Peach Jam

("Baby You're a Rich Man")

This simple, sweet, and tangy jam will keep your Beatles breakfast humming and really make you feel like "one of the beautiful people"!

INGREDIENTS
3 cups (825 ml) peeled and
   chunked ripe peaches
1 cup (275 ml) sugar
2 tablespoons lemon juice

EQUIPMENT
Gallon-sized (3.8 l) microwave-
   safe bowl
Covered 2-quart (1.9 l) container

Microwave the peaches and sugar uncovered on high in the microwave-safe bowl for 5 minutes. Stir and mash the peaches well, and then microwave uncovered on high for another 8 minutes. Stir again and microwave one last time, uncovered on high, for 2 to 4 minutes or until the jam has thickened. Remove from the microwave and stir in half of the lemon juice to start, adding more to taste. Let cool, then refrigerate in a covered container. Serve cold on English muffins, bagels, toast, Happiness Is a Warm Bun buns (page 5), or All Things Must Pass Bran Muffins (page 3). Makes about 1½ cups (355 ml) of jam.

Did you know . . . ?

🍎 According to the Recording Industry Association of America (RIAA), the Beatles have had the most number one singles of all time, with twenty-two; the most number one albums of all time, with eighteen; the most platinum albums of all time, with thirty-three; and the most multiplatinum disks of all time, with twenty.

Frittata as a Bird

("Free as a Bird")

This scrumptious broccoli omelet with an Italian flair makes a fabulous brunch or light lunch. In fact, eating this frittata is the *next . . . best . . . thing* to being . . . well, you know the rest!

INGREDIENTS
1 tablespoon salted butter
2 tablespoons minced onion
1 garlic clove, minced
1 10-ounce (285 g) package chopped broccoli, thawed
¼ teaspoon oregano
4 medium eggs

Salt and black pepper to taste
¼ cup (70 ml) grated mozzarella cheese

EQUIPMENT
Large skillet
Mixing bowl

Heat the butter in a large skillet. Add the minced onion and garlic and sauté together for 2 minutes. Add the chopped broccoli and cook until the broccoli is tender, but not soft. Stir in the oregano. In a mixing bowl, beat the eggs with a fork until they are smooth. Add salt and pepper to taste. Pour the eggs over the vegetables in the skillet and cook, covered, for 10 to 12 minutes over low heat. Do not stir the frittata as it is cooking. When the eggs are set, sprinkle with grated mozzarella and cook, covered, for 2 to 3 minutes more, until the cheese melts. Remove from the heat and let stand for 2 minutes before cutting. Serve for brunch or lunch with buttered toast. Serves 2 to 3.

Did you know . . . ?

🍎 When Ringo first heard the completed version of "Free as a Bird," he exclaimed, "It sounds like the bloody Beatles!"

Polythene Pamcakes

("Polythene Pam")

Recipe title notwithstanding, these delicious pancakes don't have even a hint of petrochemical additives.

INGREDIENTS
- 2 medium eggs, separated
- 1 cup (235 ml) buttermilk
- 2 tablespoons (¼ stick) salted butter, melted
- 1 tablespoon sugar
- ½ teaspoon baking soda
- 1 cup (275 ml) all-purpose flour
- ½ teaspoon salt
- ½ teaspoon baking powder

EQUIPMENT
2 small bowls (to separate eggs)
Large mixing bowl
Griddle or skillet

Beat the egg yolks. Beat the egg whites until stiff. In a large bowl, combine the egg yolks, buttermilk, and butter. Sift together the sugar, baking soda, flour, salt, and baking powder, and beat this dry mixture into the egg yolk mixture. Finally, fold in the egg whites.

Ladle the batter onto a hot griddle or into a skillet in which a little butter has been melted. Cook over low flame until golden brown on each side. Makes 12 to 16 pancakes, depending on their size.

Did you know . . . ?

🍎 In the *Abbey Road* song "The End," John, Paul, and George take turns playing a guitar solo. They each play precisely one bar at a time; the play order is Paul, George, and John.

Oat Days a Week

("Eight Days a Week")

These delicious spiced oat cookies—which are perfect for a light breakfast—are so good you'll want to have them eight days a week.

INGREDIENTS
½ cup (1 stick) salted butter
½ cup (140 ml) vegetable shortening
1¾ cups (210 ml) all-purpose flour
½ cup (140 ml) granulated sugar
½ cup (140 ml) packed brown sugar
1 medium egg
1 teaspoon cinnamon
½ teaspoon baking soda

½ teaspoon vanilla extract
¼ teaspoon ground nutmeg
¼ teaspoon ground cloves
1 cup (275 ml) quick-cooking rolled oats
½ cup (140 ml) toasted sliced almonds, finely chopped

EQUIPMENT
Large mixing bowl
Electric mixer
Wax paper
Large baking sheet

In a large bowl, beat together the butter and vegetable shortening with an electric mixer on high for 30 seconds. Add half of the all-purpose flour to the bowl, along with the sugars, egg, cinnamon, baking soda, vanilla, nutmeg, and cloves. Beat well until all the ingredients are combined. Add the remaining flour and stir in the rolled oats.

Shape this batter into 2 7-inch (18 cm) rolls. Wrap the rolls in wax paper and refrigerate for at least 6 hours but no longer than 24 hours (they'll dry out if refrigerated longer). Remove the wax paper and cut each of the rolls into 30 1/4-inch (6 mm) slices.

Preheat the oven to 375° F (190° C). Place the cookies 1 inch (25 mm) apart on a large baking sheet. Bake for 8 to 9 minutes, until the edges are golden brown. Remove from the oven; cool the cookies for 1 minute on the sheet. Remove the cookies from the sheet and allow to completely cool. Makes 60 cookies.

Crumb Together

("Come Together")

Here come old flattop . . . and the reason he stopped by is for a piece of this delightful cherry crumb cake!

INGREDIENTS

CRUMB CAKE
- ¾ *cup (210 ml) sugar*
- ¼ *cup (70 ml) vegetable shortening*
- 1 *medium egg*
- ½ *teaspoon almond extract*
- ½ *cup (120 ml) milk*
- 2 *cups (550 ml) all-purpose sifted flour*
- 2 *teaspoons baking powder*
- ½ *teaspoon salt*
- 2 *cups (550 ml) canned cherry pie filling*

STREUSEL CRUMB TOPPING
- ½ *cup (140 ml) sugar*
- ½ *teaspoon cinnamon*
- ⅓ *cup (90 ml) all-purpose flour*
- ¼ *cup (½ stick) salted butter, softened*

EQUIPMENT
Large mixing bowl
2 medium mixing bowls
9 × 9 inch (23 × 23 cm) baking pan

Preheat the oven to 375° F (190° C). In a large mixing bowl, combine the sugar, vegetable shortening, egg, and almond extract. Stir in the milk. In another bowl, sift together the flour, baking powder, and salt. Stir this mixture into the sugar-and-egg mixture in the first bowl. Finally, blend in the 2 cups of cherry pie filling.

Make the topping: In a mixing bowl, combine the sugar, cinnamon, flour, and soft butter. Mix until crumbly.

Grease and flour the square baking pan. Spread the batter in the pan evenly and sprinkle with the Streusel Crumb Topping. Bake for 45 to 50 minutes. Makes 1 9-inch (23 cm) crumb cake.

Culinary Collectibles

Beatles memorabilia is an industry unto itself.

Since the Fabs first became popular in the early 1960s, there has been an endless flow of Beatles-related merchandise, ranging from records and CDs (of course) to the more esoteric items like Beatles wigs, inflatable Beatles, and Beatles mobiles.

Staying on topic, though, this feature looks at some of the *food-related* Beatles memorabilia available out there, including a candy bar called a Ringo Roll. I mean, I love the Beatles and all, but I think I'd have a hard time taking a bite out of *that* particular rarity, if you know what I mean!

NOTE: Many of these items are now available only as (often very expensive) collectibles. Some Beatles food-related items, though, can often be found through memorabilia dealers and at novelty and nostalgia stores. Check the Beatlefest catalog (1-800-BEATLES), as well as the Internet, if you absolutely *must* have a Beatles tablecloth for your next dinner party.

- A stuffed apple given out as an Apple promotional item.
- A brass apple inscribed FRESH FROM APPLE and given out as a promotional item.
- A Beatles apron in two styles: The U.S. version had the Beatles' faces embossed on it in black and white; the U.K. version had the boys in red, white, and black.
- Beatles cake decorations, consisting of 2-inch (5 cm) models of the Beatles wearing blue suits.
- Many types of Beatles ceramic coffee cups and mugs.
- Several different versions of Beatles bubblegum cards.
- Beatles bubblegum machines filled with Beatles toys.
- "Beatle Bar" ice cream bars.
- Several different types of Beatles lunch boxes with matching thermoses.
- Several different types of Beatles ceramic and plastic dishes, bowls, and saucers.
- "Ringo Roll" candy bar.
- Several types of Beatles tablecloths.
- Several types of Beatles tea sets.
- Several types of Beatles serving trays.
- The Beatles *"Yesterday" . . . and Today* "Butcher Cover" poster.
- A Beatles plastic picnic satchel.
- Various restaurant menus signed by the Beatles.
- A "Chocolate Beetle" candy bar from Hamburg.
- A glass apple paperweight.

Apple Corps
Appetizers and
Sandwiches

Mean Mr. Mustard Dip

("Mean Mr. Mustard")

John wrote "Mean Mr. Mustard" in India, so I suppose substituting curry for mustard powder would be more in keeping with the genesis of the song, right? On second thought, don't even consider that suggestion; let's draw the line at "condiments as a metaphor." Mustard powder will do just fine!

INGREDIENTS
- ½ small carrot
- ½ small onion
- ¼ green pepper
- 4 parsley sprigs
- 2 tablespoons red wine vinegar
- 1 cup (235 ml) mayonnaise
- ½ cup (120 ml) cottage cheese
- ¼ teaspoon salt
- ½ teaspoon dry mustard

EQUIPMENT
Large mixing bowl

Chop very fine the carrot, onion, pepper, and parsley, and place the mixture in a large mixing bowl. Add the vinegar, mayonnaise, cottage cheese, salt, and dry mustard. Mix well. Chill and serve as a dip for chilled fresh vegetables such as sliced cucumbers, sliced celery, carrot sticks, turnip sticks, and cauliflower florets. This also makes a delicious dip for seasoned bread sticks or Biscuits to Ride (page 17). Makes 2 cups (475 ml).

Shrimp Toast and Shout

("Twist and Shout")

The Beatles' rendition of "Twist and Shout" was an extremely popular number during their live-performing years. The Fabs often made it their closing number—not necessarily for effect, but because John used to literally scream the lyrics, and his voice would be shot after singing it. The Beatles' "Twist and Shout" was one of the highlights of the 1986 movie *Ferris Bueller's Day Off,* in which Ferris (Matthew Broderick) lip-synced the song during a parade. (Paul was reportedly peeved that the movie's producers had overdubbed brass on the track: In February 1988 he told *Musician* magazine, "If [the song] had needed brass, we'd have stuck it on ourselves.") Indeed.

Like the song, this delicious shrimp toast recipe will certainly make you and your fellow paraders twist with delight and shout with joy!

INGREDIENTS
12 slices white bread
1 pound (450 g) fresh shrimp, chopped very fine
¼ cup (70 ml) fine-chopped onion
1½ teaspoons salt
1 teaspoon sugar
1 tablespoon cornstarch
1 medium egg, beaten

1 5¼-ounce (150 g) can water chestnuts, drained and chopped fine
Olive oil for deep-frying

EQUIPMENT
Large mixing bowl
Large deep skillet
Tongs or long fork
Paper towels

Trim the crusts from the bread slices and allow the slices to slightly dry out. Mix the chopped shrimp, onion, salt, sugar, and cornstarch. (Be sure to mix well.) Add the beaten egg and water chestnuts and mix well. Spread the mixture evenly on the 12 slices of bread, then cut each slice into 4 triangle-shaped pieces. Heat 1 inch (25 mm) of olive oil in a deep skillet. Drop the bread pieces into the oil, shrimp-side down, and fry until the edges of the bread begin to turn brown. Turn the pieces over and fry until golden brown. Remove the toast from the oil and drain well on paper towels. Serve as an appetizer. Makes 48 pieces.

Biscuits to Ride

("Ticket to Ride")

These crunchy pepper biscuits go wonderfully with cheese and wine; they're also great to dip in Mean Mr. Mustard Dip (page 15). A word of caution, though: Keep a beverage handy!

INGREDIENTS
3½ cups (965 ml) all-purpose
    flour
  4 teaspoons baking powder
1½ teaspoons salt
  1 tablespoon (or more) black
    pepper

¾ cup (180 ml) olive oil
1⅛ cups (265 ml) water

EQUIPMENT
Large mixing bowl
Ungreased baking sheet

Preheat the oven to 450° F (232° C). Mix all of the ingredients thoroughly in a large bowl until the consistency is thick. Roll out the dough in long strips and cut into bite-sized (or larger) pieces. Bake on an ungreased baking sheet for 25 to 30 minutes. Makes a large bowlful of pepper biscuits.

A scarf helps, but some Fondue to You sure warms the heart.
(Photo courtesy of Photofest)

Fondue to You

("From Me to You")

Did you know that the Beatles loved this recipe so much that the original chorus of "From Me to You" went, "Just call on me and I'll send it along / With love, fondue to you"?
Really.

INGREDIENTS

- ½ *pound (225 g) Swiss cheese, cut into small pieces*
- ½ *pound (225 g) Gruyère cheese, cut into small pieces*
- 3 *tablespoons all-purpose flour*
- 2 *cups (475 ml) chicken bouillon* or *dry white wine*
  Black pepper

Crispy French bread, cut into cubes and speared on toothpicks

EQUIPMENT

Large mixing bowl
Large skillet
Wooden spoon
Toothpicks

Mix the Swiss and Gruyère cheeses with the flour in the large mixing bowl. Pour the chicken bouillon (or wine) into a large skillet and heat until hot but not boiling. Slowly add small handfuls of the cheese pieces to the liquid, stirring continuously with a wooden spoon in a figure-8 pattern until the cheese is of a smooth, dipping consistency. Remove from the heat. Sprinkle the fondue with black pepper and either serve immediately or keep warm in a fondue heater. Dunk the speared bread cubes into the fondue. Other tasty "dippers" include raw celery, carrots, strips of green pepper, cauliflower florets, cooked mushrooms, apple slices, cooked cocktail sausages, and french fries. Serves 2 to 4.

P.S. I Stuffed You

("P.S. I Love You")

This tuna-stuffed egg appetizer is so good your guests will keep "coming home to you"—for more P.S. I Stuffed You eggs!

INGREDIENTS
12 hard-boiled medium eggs, cut in half lengthwise
6 parsley sprigs
2 6½-ounce (185 g) cans solid white tuna, drained
8 ounces (225 g) cream cheese
½ cup (1 stick) salted butter, melted
2 tablespoons chopped black olives

Black pepper to taste
Garlic powder to taste (optional)
Lettuce leaves for presentation
4 tomatoes, sliced
2 lemons, sliced

EQUIPMENT
2 large mixing bowls
Food processor or blender

Remove the yolks from all 24 egg halves. Place the 24 egg whites in a bowl of cold water to prevent them from drying out and getting hard. In a food processor or blender, puree the 12 egg yolks, parsley, tuna, cream cheese, butter, and chopped olives. Season this mixture to taste with black pepper (freshly ground is best) and garlic powder, if you wish. Remove the egg whites from the water, drain them well, and spoon a bit of the stuffing mixture into the hollow of each egg half. Arrange the lettuce leaves on a serving dish and lay the stuffed eggs on top. Garnish with the tomato and lemon slices. Makes 24 stuffed egg appetizers.

Did you know . . . ?

🍎 John Lennon's first wife, Cynthia, once had a restaurant in London called (no big surprise) Lennon's. I'm not sure if she served these stuffed eggs to her patrons.

P.S. I Stuffed You Again

("P.S. I Love You")

Here's another stuffed egg appetizer recipe, only this one is a little spicier (as well as being smaller and a little easier to prepare). It doesn't have tuna.

INGREDIENTS

6 *hard-boiled medium eggs,*
  cut in half lengthwise
1 *teaspoon wine vinegar*
1 *teaspoon dry mustard*
½ *teaspoon salt*
½ *teaspoon Worcestershire*
  sauce

¼ *cup (60 ml) mayonnaise*
  Lettuce leaves for
  presentation
  Paprika

EQUIPMENT
2 large mixing bowls

Remove the yolks from all 12 egg halves. Place the 12 egg whites in a bowl of cold water to prevent them from drying out and getting hard. In a large bowl, mash together the 6 egg yolks, vinegar, dry mustard, salt, Worcestershire sauce, and mayonnaise. Spoon this mixture into the 12 egg halves, arrange on fresh lettuce leaves, and sprinkle generously with paprika. Makes 12 stuffed egg appetizers.

English Army Artichoke Dip

("A Day in the Life")

Did you hear? The English army just won the war! And do you know why? Because they were all fortified with this tantalizing artichoke dip.

INGREDIENTS
- 1 *10-ounce (285 g) can artichoke hearts, drained and chopped fine*
- 1 *cup (235 ml) mayonnaise*
- ½ *cup (140 ml) grated Parmesan cheese*

Nonstick vegetable cooking spray

EQUIPMENT
Large mixing bowl
Medium casserole baking dish

Preheat the oven to 350° F (177° C). In a large mixing bowl, blend the artichoke hearts, mayonnaise, and grated cheese. Spray a medium casserole dish with vegetable cooking spray. Pour the dip mixture into the casserole dish and bake for 40 minutes. Serve at room temperature with crackers and bread sticks, or as a dip for raw vegetables. Serves 4 to 6.

Rosetta's Roasted Pepper Spread

("Get Back," LP version)

The charming Rosetta is only mentioned on the *Let It Be* LP version of "Get Back." Know why? Rosetta was laying low so she wouldn't have to share this delicious roasted pepper spread with Jojo or Sweet Loretta Martin. (She gets it while she can!)

INGREDIENTS
1 *7-ounce (200 g) jar sweet roasted peppers, drained*
1 *tablespoon mayonnaise*
1 *8-ounce (225 g) package cream cheese, softened*
   Salt to taste

EQUIPMENT
Paper towels
Medium mixing bowl

Drain the roasted peppers thoroughly and pat them dry with paper towels to absorb all the moisture. Chop the peppers very fine. In a mixing bowl, beat together the mayonnaise, cream cheese, and salt to taste. Stir in the peppers. Chill and serve with crackers and bread sticks. Serves 2 to 6, depending on the appetites in Pepperland at the time.

Gibraltar Balls

("The Ballad of John and Yoko")

These fabulous Spanish olive and cheese appetizers will have your guests talking in their beds for a week! (About how good these balls are. Get it?)

INGREDIENTS
4 ounces (115 g) shredded sharp cheddar cheese
¼ cup (½ stick) salted butter, softened
¾ cup (210 ml) sifted all-purpose flour
⅛ teaspoon salt

½ teaspoon paprika
36 small Spanish olives

EQUIPMENT
Medium mixing bowl
Baking sheet
Toothpicks

Preheat the oven to 400° F (205° C). In a bowl, blend together the cheddar cheese, butter, flour, salt, and paprika until the mixture is the consistency of a soft dough. Shape 1 teaspoon of this mixture around each Spanish olive and arrange them on a baking sheet. Bake for 12 to 15 minutes and serve on a platter with toothpicks to spear the balls. Makes 36 Gibraltar Balls.

Did you know . . . ?

🍎 John composed the beautiful *Abbey Road* ballad "Because" after hearing Yoko play Beethoven's "Moonlight Sonata." John asked her to play it backward, and thus "Because" was born.

I Don't Want to Spoil the Patties

("I Don't Want to Spoil the Party")

These delightfully different baked mushroom burgers will guarantee your party won't be spoiled! Potato chips and bottles of beer or soda help finish off the merriment.

INGREDIENTS

1   10½-oz (310 ml) can
     condensed cream of
     mushroom soup
1½ pounds (675 g) ground
     sirloin
 ½ cup (140 ml) Italian-flavored
     dry bread crumbs
 1 medium egg, slightly beaten
 ¼ cup (70 ml) chopped onion
 ⅛ teaspoon garlic powder
 ½ cup (120 ml) water
     Black pepper

FIXINGS

Thick hamburger rolls (Italian
     hard rolls work well)
Sharp cheddar cheese slices
Lettuce
Tomato slices
Mayonnaise

EQUIPMENT
Large mixing bowl
12 × 8 × 2 inch (30 × 20 × 5 cm)
baking dish

Preheat the oven to 350° F (177° C). Mix a quarter of the soup with all of the ground sirloin, bread crumbs, egg, chopped onion, and garlic powder in a large bowl. Mix well. Shape into 6 patties and arrange in a baking dish. Bake for 30 minutes. Mix the remaining soup with the water and pour over the burgers. (Do not saturate.) Sprinkle black pepper to taste on the burgers. Bake for 10 minutes more. Serve on hard rolls with sliced cheddar cheese, lettuce, tomato, and mayonnaise. Makes 6 1/4-pound (115 g) burgers.

Hey Corn Dog

("Hey Bulldog")

In "Hey Bulldog," we learn that "some kind of happiness is measured out in miles." I think John and Paul were writing about miles of these corn dogs.

INGREDIENTS
- 8 hot dogs
- 1 cup (275 ml) all-purpose flour
- ⅔ cup (185 ml) cornmeal
- 2 tablespoons sugar
- 1½ teaspoons baking powder
- ½ teaspoon dry mustard
- 1 medium egg, beaten
- ¾ cup (180 ml) milk
- 2 tablespoons corn oil
- Corn oil for deep-frying
- 8 hot dog buns

Ketchup
Mustard
Shredded American cheese

EQUIPMENT
Paper towels
8 wooden skewers
Large mixing bowl
Small mixing bowl
Large skillet
Frying thermometer
Tongs

Remove any excess moisture from the hot dogs with paper towels. Insert a wooden skewer in one end of each hot dog, pushing it halfway into the length of the dog. Set the hot dogs aside. In a large mixing bowl, combine the flour, cornmeal, sugar, baking powder, and dry mustard. In a separate bowl, mix the egg, milk, and corn oil. Add this mixture to the dry ingredients in the first bowl and mix well until the batter is thick. Coat each hot dog in the corn batter. Pour corn oil 3/4 inch (19 mm) deep in a large skillet and heat until a frying thermometer reads 375° F (190° C). Cook 3 hot dogs at a time in the oil. Turn each hot dog with tongs after 10 seconds to secure the cooked batter to it. Cook each hot dog for 3 minutes more, turning halfway through the cooking. Place the dogs in hot dog buns and top with ketchup, mustard, and a handful of shredded American cheese. Serve with You've Got to Fry Your Love Away french fries (page 157). Makes 8 corn dogs.

Lovely Pita

("Lovely Rita")

Did you know that the original lyrics of "Lovely Rita" were supposed to be "When are you free to have a pita with me"? Well, that's what I heard. It was probably this delicious shrimp pita sandwich that Paul was offering to share with the lovely Rita.

INGREDIENTS
- 2 ounces (60 g) small cooked shrimp
- ¼ cup (70 ml) shredded lettuce
- ¼ cup (70 ml) grated sharp cheddar cheese
- 3 tablespoons grated carrot
- 2 teaspoons honey
- 2 teaspoons lemon juice
- ¼ cup (60 ml) mayonnaise
- 1 small sandwich-sized pita
  Alfalfa sprouts for garnish

EQUIPMENT
Large mixing bowl

In a large bowl, toss the shrimp, lettuce, cheddar cheese, grated carrot, honey, lemon juice, and mayonnaise. Stuff the pita with the salad and garnish the top with alfalfa sprouts. Serve with potato chips. Makes 1 sandwich.

Did you know . . . ?

🍎 In the song "Lovely Rita" on *Sgt. Pepper's Lonely Hearts Club Band*, John, Paul, and George all play comb and toilet paper. The Beatles' producer George Martin once said of this incident, "Then we were all in the bathroom, tearing up toilet paper to make the right sound through the comb. The Beatles had the luxury of being able to spend an hour of their recording time getting the right combs and right strength of toilet tissue." (By the way, the fabulous honky-tonk piano break in the middle of "Lovely Rita" was written and performed by George Martin.)

We'd Like to Take You Home With Hummus

("Sgt. Pepper's Lonely Hearts Club Band")

Hummus is a little like water—how it's going to taste depends a lot on what you put in it. This really flavorful hummus spread is perfect for a mellow *Sgt. Pepper* listening party. You'll love to take it home.

INGREDIENTS
- 4 ounces (115 g) chickpeas, soaked overnight and drained
- 1 large onion, chopped
- 1 garlic clove, chopped
- ½ cup (120 ml) plain yogurt
- 2 teaspoons lemon juice
- 1 tablespoon olive oil
- ½ teaspoon ground cumin
- Salt to taste
- 1 10-ounce (285 g) loaf French bread (optional)

EQUIPMENT
Medium saucepan
Food processor or blender

Place the drained chickpeas in a saucepan and add enough water to just cover them. Add the chopped onion and garlic and bring it all to a boil. Simmer for at least 1 hour, until the chickpeas are tender. Drain the water and pour the mixture into a food processor or blender. Puree until it is smooth. Add to this mixture the yogurt, lemon juice, olive oil, and cumin. Add salt to taste and puree again briefly to mix everything together. Remove from the food processor and chill overnight before serving. Spread on slices of French bread and serve as an appetizer. Serves 4.

*George loved We'd Love to Take You Home With Hummus so much
he'd resort to disguising himself in order to get a second helping.
(Photo courtesy of Photofest)*

Yellow Submarine Sandwich

("Yellow Submarine")

In the town where I was born . . . submarine sandwiches are like their own food group. This *enormous* Italian sandwich will surely have you singing, "We all love our yellow submarine sandwich"!

INGREDIENTS

 1 10-ounce (285 g) loaf Italian bread
 ¼ cup (60 ml) Italian oil-and-vinegar salad dressing
 6 large lettuce leaves
 12 slices cold cuts: 2 salami, 2 pepperoni, 2 boiled ham, 2 prosciutto, 2 bologna, 2 olive loaf
 6 slices cheese: 2 American, 2 provolone, 1 Swiss, 1 mozzarella
 2 medium tomatoes, sliced
 6 slices Bermuda onion
 1 tablespoon mustard
 1 tablespoon mayonnaise
 2 tablespoons chopped black olives
 6 pickle slices
 Salt and black pepper to taste
 Garlic powder to taste

EQUIPMENT
Bread knife

Slice the loaf of Italian bread open lengthwise. Spread half of the salad dressing evenly onto each half of the open loaf (reserve the remaining dressing). Layer the lettuce on the bottom half of the loaf. Layer the meat, cheese, tomatoes, and onion on top of the lettuce, overlapping the slices and arranging them in any order you like. Spread the mayonnaise and mustard on the layers as desired. Sprinkle the chopped olives on top of all the layers, top off with the pickle slices, and drizzle the remaining salad dressing on both the meat side and the bread side of the loaf. Sprinkle on salt, pepper, and garlic powder to taste. Close the loaf and cut in half. Serve with potato chips and beer or soda. Serves 1 Italian or 2 non-Italians.

"This is good, but I'd rather have a Yellow Submarine Sandwich."
(Photo courtesy of Photofest)

Cold Turkey Club Sandwich
("Cold Turkey")

John wrote "Cold Turkey" about kicking heroin. Bet he was hungry when he came out the other side and, boy oh boy, would this triple-decker sandwich have hit the spot!

INGREDIENTS
 Salted butter
 2 tablespoons Miracle Whip
 3 slices white bread, toasted crisp
 4 slices cooked turkey breast
 Salt
 Black pepper
 3 slices tomato

 3 slices bacon, fried crisp and drained
 Green olives
 Pickle slices
 Potato chips

EQUIPMENT
 Bread knife

Spread butter and Miracle Whip on one side of one slice of toast. Cover this slice with sliced turkey and sprinkle the turkey with salt and pepper. Spread butter and Miracle Whip on both sides of the second slice of toast and place this slice on top of the turkey. On this slice, place the tomato and bacon slices; season with salt and pepper. Spread butter and Miracle Whip on one side of the last slice of toast and place this slice, buttered-side down, on top of the tomato and bacon slices. Cut the sandwich into triangular quarters and stick a toothpick into each quarter, if desired, to keep it together until eaten. Serve with green olives, pickle slices, and potato chips. Serves 1.

Did you know . . . ?

- At a press conference in 1964 John Lennon said that he felt the Beatles' success would only last another five years. John was both right and wrong: The Beatles *as a group* did last only another five or six years; the Beatles' *success,* however, has endured even to the present, more than three decades later.

Wings' Wings
(Wings)

Paul once said, "My philosophy of a band is, if you can play your stuff in a pub, then you're a good band." In 1973 Paul and his post-Beatles group Wings went on a tour of universities, playing live before college audiences. While not actually a pub environment, this did present the same kind of intimate feel that playing before a small audience provides. As we all know, Buffalo wings are a favorite bar food in pubs, and so this recipe is dedicated to those days when Paul took his Wings show on the road in his (ultimately successful) attempt to return (at least symbolically) to his Beatles touring roots.

INGREDIENTS
- ½ cup (120 ml) melted salted butter
- ¼ cup (60 ml) hot pepper sauce
  Ground red pepper to taste
  Corn oil for deep-frying
- 15 chicken wings, each broken into 2 sections

Celery sticks
Ranch dip

EQUIPMENT
Large mixing bowl
Large skillet
Frying thermometer

Preheat the oven to 300° F (150 ° C). In a large mixing bowl, combine the melted butter, hot pepper sauce, and ground red pepper to taste, and stir well. Heat 1/2 to 1 inch (13 to 25 mm) of corn oil in a large skillet until it registers 400° F (205° C). Pat dry the chicken wings and deep-fry them for approximately 12 minutes or until they are cooked through and the skin is crispy. As you remove the cooked wings from the oil, toss them in the pepper sauce to coat each one thoroughly. Keep the wings warm in the oven until all are cooked. Serve with celery sticks and ranch dip (and a *cold* beverage of choice). Makes 30 Wings' Wings.

Being for the Bruschetta of Mr. Kite!

("Being for the Benefit of Mr. Kite!")

This is an absolutely irresistible, garlicky toasted bread and vegetable appetizer contributed by the renowned chef Erik "Tee-Tee" von Leeming Sr. A caution: No matter how much of this bruschetta you make, it will not be enough. It is so tasty that "a splendid time is guaranteed for all" who are lucky enough to partake of it!

INGREDIENTS

2 large tomatoes, diced small
1 bunch scallions, chopped
1 teaspoon dried basil
1 8-ounce (235 ml) bottle
   Italian salad dressing
   (oil-and-vinegar based,
   not creamy)
¼ cup (½ stick) salted butter
¼ cup (60 ml) olive oil
4 garlic cloves, minced
2 tablespoons parsley

1 16-ounce (450 g) loaf
   French bread
   Grated Parmesan cheese
8 ounces (225 g) shredded
   mozzarella cheese

EQUIPMENT

Large mixing bowl
Large skillet
Large cookie sheet
Pastry brush

Preheat the broiler. In a large bowl, combine the diced tomatoes, scallions, basil, and salad dressing, and toss well. Chill.

In a large skillet, melt the butter. Add the olive oil and minced garlic and sauté until the garlic is soft. Add the parsley to the skillet, stir, and continue to sauté over low heat.

Cut the loaf of French bread into 28 to 30 1/2-inch (13 mm) wide diagonal slices. Lay the slices flat on a large cookie sheet and use a pastry brush to spread some of the hot butter-and-oil mixture onto each slice. Sprinkle with grated Parmesan. Cover each slice with a liberal amount of the shredded mozzarella.

Place the bread slices under the broiler until the mozzarella melts and turns brown around the edges. Remove the bread from the oven and place 1 tablespoon of the chilled tomatoes and scallion mixture on top of each slice. Serve immediately. Makes 28 to 30 slices; serves 6 to 8.

Beer Prudence

("Dear Prudence")

"Dear Prudence," which was written by John in India for Mia Farrow's sister Prudence, has one of the greatest bass lines Paul McCartney ever recorded. Here's a suggestion: Make up a batch of this terrific fondue, program your CD player to repeat "Dear Prudence" ad infinitum, and let the song play until the fondue is all gone.

INGREDIENTS
- 2 tablespoons (¼ stick) salted butter
- 1 garlic clove, crushed
- 2 tablespoons all-purpose flour
- 2 tablespoons Worcestershire sauce
- 1½ teaspoons dry mustard
- ¼ teaspoon caraway seeds
- ⅛ teaspoon cayenne
- 8 ounces (225 g) extra-sharp cheddar cheese, grated
- 8 ounces (235 ml) beer

EQUIPMENT
Fondue pot
Fondue warmer

Heat the butter in a fondue pot. Sauté the garlic in the pot over low heat until it's soft. Add the flour to the pot and stir continuously until smooth. Add the Worcestershire sauce, dry mustard, caraway seeds, cayenne, cheddar cheese, and beer to the pot and stir continuously until the mixture is smooth and creamy. Transfer the fondue pot to the fondue warmer and serve as a dip for bread sticks, raw celery, carrots, strips of green pepper, cauliflower florets, cooked mushrooms, apple slices, cooked cocktail sausages, and french fries. Serves 2 to 4.

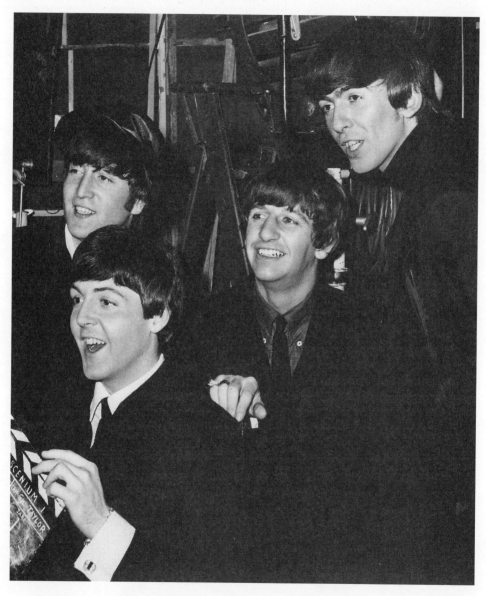

Nearly thirty years after their breakup, the Beatles still star in the hearts of their fans. (Photo courtesy of Photofest)

Beatlemania
Breads

She Said . . . Spinach Bread!

("She Said, She Said")

The reason she said "spinach bread" was that she had gotten a taste of this incredible stuffed bread and couldn't wait to have some more.

INGREDIENTS
- 1 pound (450 g) ready-to-bake bread dough, thawed
- 1 10-ounce (285 g) package frozen spinach, thawed
- 1 4-ounce (115 g) can black olives, chopped small
- 1 tablespoon olive oil
- 3 tablespoons grated cheese of your choice (I like zesty Romano, but Parmesan works just as well)

Salt and black pepper to taste

EQUIPMENT
Rolling pin
Large mixing bowl
Flat baking pan

Preheat the oven to 350° F (177° C). Roll the bread dough out flat like a pizza. In a large mixing bowl, blend the thawed spinach, olives, olive oil, grated cheese, and salt and pepper to taste; mix well. Spread the mixture evenly on the bread dough and roll the dough up like a jelly roll. Bake for 30 to 35 minutes. Slice into 1/2-inch (13 mm) slices and serve hot or at room temperature as an appetizer or as an accompaniment to pasta. Makes 1 loaf.

Did you know . . . ?

 There is a total of 35,390 written words in all of the Beatles' songs, divided among 2,346 distinct words. If written in standard double-spaced manuscript form, with 300 words per page, these words would make up approximately 108 pages of text.

Thanks for the Pepperoni Bread

("Thanks for the Pepperoni")

Okay, so George's *All Things Must Pass* track "Thanks for the Pepperoni" is a somewhat obscure "Beatles" tune to reference for a recipe title. But come on: How could I resist using what may be the only song in the history of the world to actually use the word *pepperoni* in its title? Add to that the fact that this delicious Pepperoni Bread is one of the most unique culinary concoctions in this book and something I really wanted to introduce to y'all . . . and I rest my case.

INGREDIENTS
¾ cup (180 ml) milk
½ cup (120 ml) Italian salad dressing (oil-and-vinegar based, not creamy)
1 5-ounce (145 g) jar Old English cheddar cheese spread
2 medium eggs
2¾ cups (760 ml) all-purpose flour
2 tablespoons sugar
1½ teaspoons baking powder
1 teaspoon dry mustard
¼ teaspoon baking soda
1 cup (275 ml) diced pepperoni
Olive-oil-flavored nonstick vegetable cooking spray

EQUIPMENT
Electric beater
Large mixing bowl
Small mixing bowl
9 × 5 inch (23 × 13 cm) loaf pan

With an electric beater, blend together in large mixing bowl until smooth the milk, salad dressing, Old English cheese spread, and eggs. Preheat the oven to 350° F (177° C). In a separate bowl, combine the flour, sugar, and baking powder. Stir by hand into the cheese mixture the dry mustard, baking soda, pepperoni, and flour mixture. Continue blending until the batter is moist. Spray the loaf pan with olive-oil-flavored vegetable cooking spray. Pour the bread batter into the pan and bake for 50 to 55 minutes. Immediately remove the loaf from the pan and let it settle before slicing. Makes 1 loaf.

Did you know . . . ?

● It was David Crosby of Crosby, Stills, and Nash who first introduced the music of Indian sitarist Ravi Shankar to George Harrison.

Banana Bread on the Run

("Band on the Run")

Picture in your mind the *Band on the Run* album cover: Can you see it? The band Wings is spotlighted against a wall. Well, guess what? The reason the band is on the run is that they stole loaves of this delicious banana bread and they don't want to give them back! (And stop groaning! You think it's easy coming up with clever Beatles-themed intros to all these recipes?)

INGREDIENTS

- 3 *ripe bananas*
- 1 *cup (275 ml) sugar*
- ½ *cup (140 ml) vegetable shortening*
- 1 *medium egg*
- 1½ *cups (415 ml) all-purpose flour*
- 1 *teaspoon ground nutmeg*
- 1½ *teaspoon baking soda*
- 1 *teaspoon vanilla extract*

EQUIPMENT

- 9 × 5 *inch (23 × 13 cm) loaf pan*
- 2 *mixing bowls*

Preheat the oven to 350° F (177° C). Grease and flour the loaf pan. In a small bowl, mash the bananas. In a large bowl, cream together the sugar, shortening, and egg, then add the mashed bananas. Use the small bowl to blend together the flour, nutmeg, and baking soda. Gradually add this to the banana mixture. Add the vanilla to the mixture as the last step. Pour into the greased loaf pan and bake for 1 hour and 15 minutes. Makes 1 loaf.

Paperback Fritters

("Paperback Writer")

"Paperback Writer" begins with soaring harmonies and then heads right into a kick-ass guitar riff à la "Day Tripper"—except that in "Writer," the riff was recorded by an amplified and distorted *bass* guitar, not a standard six-stringer. Another Beatles first.

If you've never tasted these truly delicious corn and onion fritters, you're in for a delightful "first" as well—only in your case it'll be culinary instead of musical.

INGREDIENTS
2 cups (550 ml) cornmeal
1 tablespoon all-purpose flour
½ teaspoon baking soda
1 teaspoon baking powder
1 teaspoon salt
3 tablespoons chopped onion
1 cup (235 ml) buttermilk

1 medium egg, beaten
1½ tablespoons salted butter

EQUIPMENT
Large mixing bowl
Large skillet
Paper towels

In a large mixing bowl, combine the cornmeal, flour, baking soda, baking powder, and salt. Mix well. Stir in the chopped onion and buttermilk. Stir in the beaten egg last. Melt the butter in a large skillet. Drop spoonfuls of the fritter batter into the hot butter and fry until golden brown. Drain well on paper towels. Serve as a side dish with the Beatles-inspired main course of your choosing. Serves 4.

I Dig a Zucchini Bread

("Dig a Pony")

Well, you can celebrate anything you want . . . as long as you serve this delicious bread at the celebration!

INGREDIENTS
  3 cups (825 ml) grated
     zucchini
  1 cup (235 ml) vegetable oil
1½ cups (415 ml) sugar
  3 medium eggs, beaten
  1 teaspoon vanilla extract
  3 cups (825 ml) flour
1½ teaspoons baking powder
  1 teaspoon baking soda

1½ teaspoons cinnamon
  1 teaspoon salt
  ½ teaspoon ground ginger
     Nonstick vegetable cooking
     spray

EQUIPMENT
9 × 5 inch (23 × 13 cm) loaf pan
2 large mixing bowls

Preheat the oven to 350° F (177° C). In a large mixing bowl, combine the zucchini, vegetable oil, sugar, beaten eggs, and vanilla, and mix well. In a separate bowl, sift together the flour, baking powder, baking soda, cinnamon, salt, and ginger. Add this dry mixture to the zucchini mixture and beat together for 4 minutes. Spray the loaf pan with cooking spray. Pour the batter into the loaf pan and bake for 1 hour. Be careful not to overbake, because this will dry out the bread. Allow the bread to cool before slicing. Makes 1 loaf.

Did you know . . . ?

● In the 1960s the Beatles recorded several songs written by Bob Dylan but never released any of them. Dylan songs recorded by the Fabs included "Like a Rolling Stone," "All Along the Watchtower," "Blowin' in the Wind," "Mister Tambourine Man," "Rainy Day Women No. 12 and 35," and "It Ain't Me Babe."

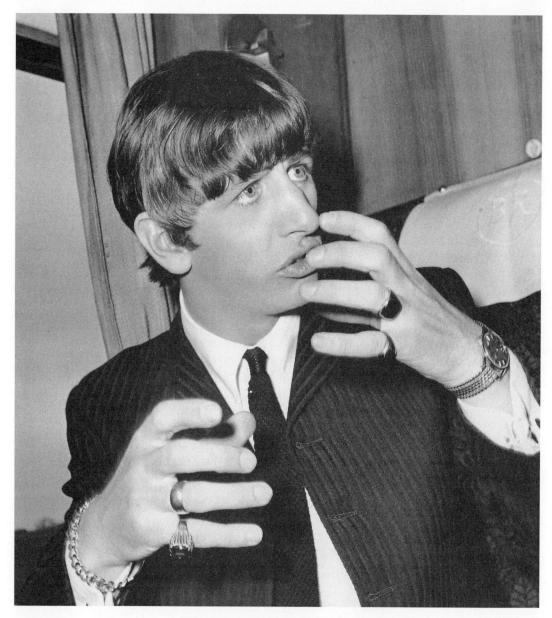

"Phew, luv, you really should brush after that Big Garlic Bread."
(Photo courtesy of Photofest)

Big Garlic Bread

("Big Barn Bed")

The inspiration for this recipe is the Wings song "Big Barn Bed," off their *Red Rose Speedway* album. Another song on that LP is "One More Kiss." As I've tried to do throughout this book, I must once again call your attention to one of the critical ingredients in this recipe: rather large quantities of garlic, also known as the "stinking rose." Trust me: If *you* would like "One More Kiss" from your beloved, attend to your odoriferous mouth after eating this delicious (but lingeringly aromatic) garlic bread!

INGREDIENTS

½ *cup (1 stick) unsalted butter*
4 *garlic cloves, crushed*
4 *tablespoons parsley*
   Juice of 1 lemon

1 *large French baguette*

EQUIPMENT
Food processor or blender
Aluminum foil

Preheat the oven to 350° F (177° C). Combine the butter, garlic, parsley, and lemon juice and puree in a food processor or blender until smooth. (Do not puree too thin.) Chill. Slice the French baguette diagonally but do not cut all the way through the loaf. Spread all the cut sides with the garlic butter. Wrap the loaf in aluminum foil. Bake for 20 minutes. Serves 4.

And I Love Herb

("And I Love Her")

The beautiful Lennon-McCartney ballad "And I Love Her" is one of the most covered Beatles songs of all time. Paul admitted in 1984 that he and John were specifically trying to write a classic like Perry Como's "And I Love Her So." Methinks they succeeded.

This flavorful bread goes wonderfully with soups or stews, or is terrific all by itself. The garlic, basil, and cheese flavors blend beautifully—especially when served warm!

INGREDIENTS
- 2 tablespoons vegetable shortening
- 2 teaspoons salt
- 2 tablespoons sugar
- 1 cup (235 ml) hot milk
- 1 cup (235 ml) hot water
- 1 package (¼ ounce/18 g) dry yeast
- ¼ cup (60 ml) warm water
- 6 cups (1,650 ml) all-purpose white flour
- 2 garlic cloves, minced
- 1 cup (275 ml) grated Parmesan cheese
- ¼ cup (70 ml) shredded provolone cheese
- 2 tablespoons dried basil, crumbled

EQUIPMENT
Large mixing bowl
Small mixing bowl
Large cutting board (floured)
Large bowl (greased)
2 large loaf pans

In a large bowl, mix the vegetable shortening, salt, and sugar. Add the hot milk and hot water and allow the mixture to cool to lukewarm.

In a small bowl, mix the yeast with the warm water and let it stand for 5 minutes to dissolve completely. Add the dissolved yeast and half of the flour to the first mixture and beat well until it is thoroughly blended. Add to this 2 cups of the remaining flour, along with the garlic, Parmesan, provolone, and dried basil. Mix well. Turn this batter out onto a floured cutting board and knead for 2 minutes. Let it rest for 10 minutes. Add to the batter just enough of the remaining flour so that it is not sticky. Knead the dough again until it is smooth and elastic. Place it in a large, greased bowl and cover.

Allow the dough to rise in a warm spot until it doubles in size. Remove the dough from the bowl, punch it down, and shape it into 2 loaves. Place each loaf in a large, greased loaf pan and again allow them to double in size.

Preheat the oven to 425° F (218° C). Bake the loaves for 15 minutes. Reduce the oven temperature to 375° F (190° C) and bake the loaves for 30 minutes more. Remove the loaves from the pans and allow them to cool on racks before slicing. Makes 2 loaves.

Did you know . . . ?

- According to comments made by Paul over the years, the Beatles' songs "She Loves You," "And I Love Her," "We Can Work It Out," "You Won't See Me," and "Here, There and Everywhere" were all written for his then fiancée Jane Asher.

(Photo courtesy of Photofest)

"Working for Peanuts" Bread
("Drive My Car")

One bite of this rich, peanut lover's bread will have you singing, "Beep beep, mmm, beep beep, *yeah!*"

INGREDIENTS
1¾ cups (485 ml) all-purpose
   flour
⅓ cup (90 ml) sugar
1 tablespoon baking powder
½ teaspoon salt
1 cup (235 ml) peanut butter
1 medium egg
1 cup (235 ml) milk

1 cup (275 ml) chopped
   salted peanuts

EQUIPMENT
Large mixing bowl
Small mixing bowl
9 × 5 inch (23 × 13 cm)
   loaf pan

Preheat the oven to 350° F (177° C). In a large mixing bowl, combine the flour, sugar, baking powder, and salt, and mix well. Add spoonfuls of the peanut butter to the bowl and mix well until the mixture resembles coarse crumbs. In a small bowl, beat together the egg and milk. Stir the beaten egg and milk into the flour mixture, and then stir in the chopped peanuts. Grease and flour the loaf pan and pour in the batter. Bake the bread for approximately 1 hour. Test by sticking a toothpick into the center of the loaf: When the toothpick comes out completely clean, the bread is done. Remove the loaf from the pan by inverting it over a rack. Turn it back over so that the top side is up and allow it to cool *completely* before cutting. (This bread will slice better the following day.) Makes 1 loaf or 12 to 16 servings.

Paul and Linda's Dinner With John and Yoko

Trepanning is the practice of drilling a hole in the human skull. It is performed for hoped-for enlightenment, "balancing" of bodily fluids, and, during the Middle Ages, to rid the body of possessing demons.

The following anecdote was recounted by Paul McCartney during an interview in October 1986.

Linda and me came over for dinner once and John said, "You fancy getting the trepanning thing done?" I said, "Well, what is it?" and he said, "Well, you kind of have a hole bored into your skull and it relieves the pressure."

We're sitting at dinner and this is seriously being offered!

Now this wasn't a joke, this was like, Let's go next week, we know a guy who can do it and maybe we can do it all together. So I said, "Look, you go and have it done, and if it works, great. Tell us about it and we'll all have it."

But I'm afraid I've always been a bit cynical about stuff like that—thank God!—because I think that there's so much crap that you've got to be careful of. But John was more open to things like that.

There is no evidence (to quote Paul, "Thank God!") that John Lennon ever seriously pursued the idea of having his head trepanned. He did talk about it, though.

George Harrison   Ringo Starr   Paul McCartney   John Lennon

MDN-11 (456)

Always look your best before coming to the table.
(Photo courtesy of Photofest)

"Ready, Steady, Go!"
Salads and Sauces

Tomato Never Knows

("Tomorrow Never Knows")

This classic Italian tomato and olive oil salad is perfect when you want to turn off your mind, relax, and float downstream.

INGREDIENTS
- 2 large tomatoes
- 3 tablespoons olive oil
- 1 garlic clove, sliced thin
- $\frac{1}{4}$ teaspoon salt
- $\frac{1}{4}$ teaspoon garlic powder
- $\frac{1}{4}$ teaspoon oregano
- $\frac{1}{8}$ teaspoon black pepper
- 4 thick slices mozzarella cheese

EQUIPMENT
Large serving bowl
Large mixing bowl

Wash the tomatoes and cut them into bite-sized pieces. Place them in a serving bowl and set aside. In a mixing bowl, combine the olive oil, garlic, salt, garlic powder, oregano, and pepper, and mix well. Pour this dressing mixture over the tomatoes and chill briefly before serving. Serve on top of slices of mozzarella cheese with Italian or French bread. Serves 2.

Did you know . . . ?

- The first song Neil Young ever performed for a live audience was the Beatles' "It Won't Be Long."

Love You Tuna Salad Sandwich

("Love You Too")

In the classic *Revolver* tune, George sings, "But what you've got means such a lot to me." We think you'll agree that this unique tuna salad will mean a lot to *you!*

INGREDIENTS

1 6½-ounce (185 g) can solid white tuna, drained and flaked

¼ cup (70 ml) shredded sharp cheddar cheese

¼ cup (70 ml) shredded Swiss cheese

½ cup (140 ml) finely chopped celery

3 tablespoons fine-chopped Bermuda onion

¼ cup (60 ml) mayonnaise

¼ cup (60 ml) tartar sauce Dash black pepper

6 slices pumpernickel bread Lettuce

6 slices tomato

6 slices sour pickle

6 slices rye bread

EQUIPMENT

Large mixing bowl

Combine the tuna, cheeses, celery, onion, mayonnaise, tartar sauce, and pepper in a large bowl. Mix well. Spread on the pumpernickel bread, top each slice with lettuce, tomato, and a sour pickle slice, and cover with a slice of rye. Serve with potato chips and soda. Makes 6 nice sandwiches. (For a Love You *Hot* Tuna Salad Sandwich, place the bottom halves of the sandwiches under the broiler for a couple of minutes before adding the fixings, then cover with the top slice of bread. Mmm.)

Come Together Tomato and Potato Salad

("Come Together")

This quick and tasty potato salad with a twist will leave you with plenty of time to polish your walrus gumboots and trim your Ono sideboards!

INGREDIENTS
- 1 pound (450 g) potatoes, skinned, diced, and boiled (or 1 16-ounce/450 g can sliced white potatoes, diced and heated until warm)
- 10 ounces (280 g) fresh tomato, skinned, seeded, and chopped into small pieces
- 1½ onions, chopped fine
- 3 ounces (90 g) black olives, chopped
- ¼ cup (60 ml) mayonnaise
- 2 tablespoons plus 2 teaspoons milk
  Black pepper to taste

EQUIPMENT
1 large mixing bowl
1 medium mixing bowl

In a large bowl, mix together the potato slices, tomato pieces, onions, and black olives. In a medium bowl, mix together the mayonnaise and milk, and add black pepper to taste. Toss the vegetables with the dressing mixture and chill. Serve as a cold side dish. Serves 6.

I Wilt Salad

("I Will")

Who knows how long you'll love this delicious wilted salad? Here's a suggestion: During dinner, if your host asks if anyone will be having seconds of this tasty hot salad, shout out loud, "I wilt!"

INGREDIENTS
- Lettuce to fill 2 small salad bowls
- 4 hard-boiled medium eggs, sliced
- 5 slices bacon, cut into small pieces
- ½ cup (120 ml) mild vinegar

- ½ teaspoon sugar
- ½ teaspoon chopped fresh parsley
- ½ teaspoon oregano
- 1 tablespoon chopped onion

EQUIPMENT
Medium skillet

Arrange the egg slices on top of the lettuce in the 2 bowls. Sauté the bacon in the skillet until crispy. Remove the bacon from the skillet and set aside. To the bacon drippings in the pan add the vinegar, sugar, parsley, oregano, and onion. Heat well, add the cooked bacon, heat a little longer until the bacon is warm, and pour hot over the lettuce and hard-boiled eggs. Serve immediately. Serves 2.

Heart of the Coleslaw

("Heart of the Country")

I have determined that on the *Ram* album, Paul was essentially singing about this "Heart of the Country"–inspired coleslaw. Why? Because after he performs "Heart of the Country," he tells us he wants to "Eat at Home" with his "Long-Haired Lady!" "Dear Boy," what else could he have been singing about but this incredible salad, right?

INGREDIENTS
* 4 cups (1,100 ml) shredded
  cabbage
* ½ cup (120 ml) mayonnaise
* ½ tablespoon vinegar
* ½ tablespoon lemon juice
* 1 tablespoon grated onion
* ½ teaspoon celery seeds
* 1 teaspoon sugar
* ½ teaspoon salt
* ⅛ teaspoon black pepper
  Paprika for garnish
  Green pepper rings for
  garnish

EQUIPMENT
* 2 large bowls

Soak the shredded cabbage in ice water in a large bowl until it is crisp. In a mixing bowl, combine the mayonnaise, vinegar, lemon juice, grated onion, celery seeds, sugar, salt, and pepper. Mix well. Drain the cabbage and mix well with the dressing. Garnish with paprika and green pepper rings. Serve chilled. Serves 4.

Did you know . . . ?

* Paul's father, Jim McCartney, was a professional musician with a group called the Masked Melody Makers. In 1974 Paul released a song called "Walking in the Park With Eloise," which was a combination of his father's original instrumental tune "Eloise" and Paul's lyrics. Jim McCartney died in 1976, but he was alive and active the whole time Paul was in the Beatles and for almost a decade after. Jim was one of the few Beatle parents fully able to appreciate his son's phenomenal success.

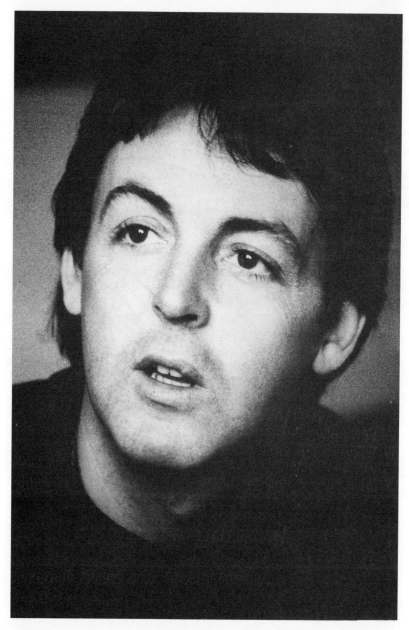

A very much alive Paul often snacks on a bowl of Cranberry Sauce.
(Photo courtesy of Photofest)

Cranberry Sauce

("Strawberry Fields Forever")

This delicious sauce is probably the recipe John was calling for at the end of "Strawberry Fields Forever." Although to be honest, it does sound like he's saying, "I buried Paul," doesn't it? Guess we'll never know (although John provides a definitive answer, of sorts, at the end of *Strawberry Fields* on *Anthology 2*!).

INGREDIENTS
12 ounces (340 g) fresh
     cranberries
 1 cup (235 ml) water
1½ cups (415 ml) sugar
     Salt

EQUIPMENT
Large kettle

Wash the cranberries. Bring the water to a boil, then add the cranberries and sugar. Cook for 10 to 12 minutes or until the skins of the cranberries pop open. Skim off the white froth that forms on top of the water. Let the sauce cool. Refrigerate. Serve cold with pork or turkey dishes. Serves 8.

If I Ever Sauced You

("I Will")

When this tangy cheese sauce is served around the table, everyone will want to be the first to say, "I will!"

INGREDIENTS
- 1 tablespoon salted butter
- 1 tablespoon all-purpose flour
- 1 cup (235 ml) hot milk
  Salt and black pepper to taste

- 2 ounces (60 g) grated sharp cheddar cheese
- 1 teaspoon prepared mustard

EQUIPMENT
Large saucepan

Melt the butter in a saucepan over medium heat. Add the flour and cook for 1 minute, stirring constantly. Do not allow the flour to brown! While continuing to stir, add the milk, bring the sauce to a boil, and simmer for 5 minutes. Add salt and pepper to taste. Remove the pan from the heat and stir in the cheddar cheese and mustard. Continue stirring until the sauce is smooth. Pour over meats, vegetables, rice—whatever you like. Makes 1 cup (235 ml).

Hello Garlic Sauce
("Hello Goodbye")

You'll say Yes! to this delightful, light "tomato-less" sauce for pasta.

INGREDIENTS
- ½ cup (120 ml) olive oil
- 2 garlic cloves, chopped
- ½ cup (120 ml) water
- 1 tablespoon parsley

- ½ teaspoon black pepper
- Salt to taste

EQUIPMENT
Large skillet

Heat the olive oil in a large skillet. Add the chopped garlic and cook until it is browned. Slowly stir in the water. Add the parsley, black pepper, and salt to taste. Simmer slowly for 10 minutes, stirring occasionally. Serve over 1 pound (450 g) of a cooked pasta of your choice. Serves 4.

Did you know . . . ?

🍎 John Lennon once said of the Beatles, "Our best work was never recorded."

If You Wear Red Clam Sauce Tonight
("Yes It Is")

This red clam sauce is so good that you may find yourself "wearing" red after indulging in a dish (or three) of pasta made with this wonderful sauce.

INGREDIENTS
- 2 tablespoons (¼ stick) salted butter
- ½ cup (140 ml) chopped onion
- 2 garlic cloves, minced
- 2 15-ounce (450 ml) cans tomato sauce with tomato pieces
- ½ teaspoon oregano
- ¼ teaspoon salt
- ⅛ teaspoon black pepper
- ¼ cup (70 ml) chopped fresh parsley
- ¼ cup (60 ml) dry white wine
- 2 6½-ounce (185 g) cans minced clams, drained
- ¼ cup (70 ml) grated Parmesan cheese

EQUIPMENT
Medium saucepan

In a medium saucepan, melt the butter. Add the onion and garlic to the skillet and cook until the onion is tender. Stir in the tomato sauce, oregano, salt, pepper, parsley, white wine, and drained clams. Simmer until heated through. Pour over 1/2 to 3/4 pound (225 to 340 g) of cooked linguine. Sprinkle grated Parmesan on the pasta and serve with a tossed salad and garlic bread. Serves 4.

"I don't have the heart to tell her that she did wear red clam sauce tonight."
(Photo courtesy of Photofest)

Another Grille

("Another Girl")

"Another Girl" appeared in the film *Help!* and included a lead guitar solo by writer Paul, who also played bass in the song.

INGREDIENTS
- 1 cup (235 ml) ketchup
- 1 tablespoon Worcestershire sauce
- 1 teaspoon garlic powder
- ¼ cup (60 ml) wine vinegar
- 1 teaspoon salt
- 1 teaspoon celery seeds
- 1 cup (235 ml) water
- 1 tablespoon sugar

EQUIPMENT
Large saucepan

In a large saucepan, combine all the ingredients. Stir well and simmer for 30 minutes. Use to baste chicken or pork ribs, or as a condiment for meats and fried potatoes. Makes approximately 2 cups (475 ml) of barbecue sauce.

Did you know . . . ?

🍎 "Norwegian Wood (This Bird Has Flown)" marked the first use of a sitar in a rock song.

Doctor Lobster

("Doctor Robert")

There's a line in "Doctor Robert" in which John tells us that "if you're down he'll pick you up." I think the same can be said for my own "Doctor Lobster": If *you're* down, this incredible sauce will most definitely pick you up!

INGREDIENTS
½ cup (120 ml) olive oil
3 garlic cloves, chopped
6 large lobster tails
1 tablespoon black pepper
1 tablespoon parsley
3 teaspoons salt
1 28-ounce (830 ml) can
crushed tomatoes

28 ounces (830 ml) water
(use empty tomato can
as a measure)

EQUIPMENT
Large saucepan

In a large saucepan, heat the olive oil. Fry the garlic in the oil until it is well cooked, then remove the garlic from the pan and discard. Place the lobster tails in the pan and cook them in the olive oil for 20 minutes. Add to the pan the black pepper, parsley, and salt, and cook for 20 minutes more. Remove the lobster tails from the pan and set aside. Add the crushed tomatoes and water to the pan and bring it to a boil. Lower the heat and simmer for 30 minutes. Return the lobster tails and cook for an additional 30 minutes, stirring occasionally. Serve over linguine or fettuccine. Serves 4 to 6.

Did you know . . . ?

🍖 The titles originally bandied about for *Revolver* were *Abracadabra, Beatles on Safari, Bubble and Squeak, Free Wheelin' Beatles,* and *Magic Circle(s).*

Potatoes to the People

("Power to the People")

Right on!

INGREDIENTS
- 4 cups (1,100 ml) boiled potatoes, cut into chunks
- ⅓ cup (75 ml) olive oil
- 3 tablespoons white vinegar
- 3 hard-boiled medium eggs, mashed
- ½ cup (140 ml) chopped onion
- 1 cup (275 ml) chopped celery
- 1 tablespoon parsley
- 1 large carrot, grated
- 1 cup (235 ml) mayonnaise
- 1 teaspoon sugar
- 1½ teaspoons salt
  - Dash black pepper

EQUIPMENT
Large mixing bowl

In a large bowl, combine all the ingredients and mix well. Chill for 1 hour before serving. If necessary, sprinkle a little cold water on the salad and mix well to improve the consistency before serving. Serves 4 to 6.

Iceberg Salad in the Dead of Night

("Blackbird")

You certainly don't have to eat this fabulous chef's salad in the "dead of night," but once your loved ones get a taste of it, that might be the only time you'll be able to enjoy it without having to share.

INGREDIENTS
- ½ head iceberg lettuce, torn into small pieces
- 1 bunch radishes, sliced
- ¼ cucumber, sliced
- 1 Bermuda onion, sliced
- 8 ounces (225 g) cooked ham, shredded
- 2 hard-boiled medium eggs, chopped
- 4 ounces (115 g) sharp cheddar cheese, cubed
- ¼ cup (60 ml) olive oil
- 2 tablespoons white wine vinegar
- Salt and black pepper to taste
- Pinch dry mustard
- Pinch sugar

EQUIPMENT
Large serving bowl
Screw-top cruet

In a large serving bowl, layer the lettuce, radishes, cucumber, onion, ham, eggs, and cheese, and toss lightly to mix. In a screw-top cruet, combine the olive oil, vinegar, salt, pepper, dry mustard, and sugar, and shake well. Pour the dressing over the salad and toss to mix. Serve immediately as a main dish with fresh Big Garlic Bread (page 45). Serves 2 to 4.

I Want to Elbow You

("I Want to Tell You")

Ted Nugent once recorded a cover version of "I Want to Tell You," the George Harrison song that inspired this delicious salad. The Beatles' version would probably make better background music, though, when you're partaking of this scrumptious chicken pasta dish.

INGREDIENTS
- 1 pound (450 g) boneless, skinless chicken breasts
- 1 large bunch fresh broccoli, trimmed, stems peeled, cut into florets
- 1 pound (450 g) elbow pasta
- 1 red bell pepper, seeded and chopped
- 3 tablespoons chopped fresh Italian parsley
  Bottled Italian oil-and-vinegar dressing
- 1 tablespoon fresh lemon juice
  Salt and black pepper to taste
- ¾ cup (210 ml) grated Parmesan cheese

EQUIPMENT
Large saucepan
Large microwave-safe bowl
Large pot
Large serving bowl

Poach the chicken in simmering, salted water until it is cooked through and no pink is visible. Remove the pot from the heat and allow the chicken to cool down in the hot water.

Microwave the broccoli until it is crisp-tender (approximately 6 minutes on high). Drain the broccoli, rinse under cold water, and set aside. Cook the elbow pasta in boiling, salted water until al dente consistency. Start testing the pasta about halfway through the cooking time suggested on the box. (The cooking times provided on pasta boxes are almost always too long. Do not overcook!) Drain the pasta, run under cold water, and drain again. Remove the cooked chicken from the water and cut it into bite-sized pieces.

In a large serving bowl, combine the chicken, elbow pasta, cooked broccoli, red bell pepper, and chopped parsley. Pour Italian dressing over the mixture to moisten to your liking. Add the lemon juice and salt and black pepper to taste and toss lightly. Sprinkle grated Parmesan on the salad before serving and provide extra grated cheese for individual salads. Serve with garlic bread. Serves 6 to 8.

Beetles and Onion Salad

(The Beatles)

This recipe is in honor of the original spelling of the Fabs' name: Yes, it was supposed to be the Beetles—as a tribute to Buddy Holly and the Crickets and other insect-inspired names of the period—until a friend of John's told him he didn't like the two *E*s and that if they spelled it "Beatles," they'd get a musical reference in the word *beat*. And so it was done and the rest is musical history.

This salad is terrific as a side dish on a hot summer's eve.

INGREDIENTS
- 2 cups (550 ml) cooked beets, chopped fine
- 1 cup (275 ml) sweet onion, chopped fine
- 2 cups (550 ml) cabbage, shredded fine
- ½ cup (120 ml) mayonnaise
  Salt and black pepper to taste

- 6 individual serving bowls of iceberg lettuce, washed (approximately 2 average-sized heads)

EQUIPMENT
Large mixing bowl

In a large mixing bowl, combine the beets, onion, and cabbage. Toss lightly. Add the mayonnaise, mix well, and season with salt and black pepper to taste. Serve over lettuce in individual salad bowls. Serves 6.

Did you know . . . ?

 According to the 1998 *Guinness Book of World Records,* the Beatles are the group with the greatest sales of any musical group in history. EMI estimates total Beatles sales at over 1 billion disks and tapes.

Eight Tomatoes a Week

("Eight Days a Week")

All together now: "Ooo, I need your tomatoes . . . guess you know it's true!"

INGREDIENTS
- 1 *pound (450 g) extra-sharp cheddar cheese, shredded*
- 5 *hard-boiled medium eggs, chopped*
- ⅓ *cup (90 ml) chopped pickles*
- ⅓ *cup (90 ml) chopped pimientos*
- ½ *cup (140 ml) green stuffed olives, chopped*
- ¾ *cup (180 ml) bottled French dressing*
  Salt and black pepper to taste
- 8 *medium tomatoes, washed and partially hollowed out*

EQUIPMENT
Large mixing bowl

In a large mixing bowl, combine the cheddar cheese, eggs, pickles, pimientos, and 3 tablespoons of the French dressing. Mix well. Season with salt and black pepper to taste. Chill. When ready to serve, spoon equal amounts of the salad into each of the 8 hollowed-out tomatoes and drizzle the remaining French dressing on top (approximately 1 tablespoon or so on each). Serve with garlic bread. Serves 8.

The Fabs would often sing for Eight Tomatoes a Week.
(Photo courtesy of Photofest)

If I Shell

("If I Fell")

The Beatles' rendition of "If I Fell" in *A Hard Day's Night* was one of the most memorable performance scenes in the movie. Here's a suggestion: After you finally get through your *own* hard day (and I know you all have them!), mix up some of these fabulous pasta-and-tuna tomato delights, put on the video of *A Hard Day's Night,* and spend *your* hard day's night with the lads from Liverpool.

INGREDIENTS
- 2 cups (550 ml) cooked shell pasta (approximately 4 ounces/115 g uncooked shells)
- ¼ pound (115 g) sharp cheddar cheese, shredded
- ¼ cup (70 ml) chopped sweet pickles
- 2 tablespoons chopped pimiento
- 1 teaspoon grated onion
- ½ cup (140 ml) diced celery
- ¼ cup (70 ml) grated carrot
- 2 6½-ounce (185 g) cans tuna in olive (or vegetable) oil, flaked
- 1½ teaspoons lemon juice
  Salt and black pepper to taste
- 12 large slices fresh tomato, not too thick
  Crisp lettuce leaves
  Miracle Whip for garnish

EQUIPMENT
Large mixing bowl
Large serving platter

In a large mixing bowl, combine the cooked pasta, cheddar cheese, pickles, pimiento, onion, celery, carrot, tuna (with the olive oil), and lemon juice, and toss well. Season with salt and black pepper to taste. On a large serving platter, lay out the lettuce leaves and 6 slices of tomato and spoon an equal amount of the macaroni-tuna salad on top of each slice. Cover each of the 6 mounds of salad with the remaining tomato slices. Spoon a dollop of Miracle Whip on top of each tomato slice and sprinkle with black pepper. Makes 6 "sandwiches."

Flew in From Miami Beam Bourbon Sauce

("Back in the U.S.S.R.")

Use enough of this bourbon-based sauce and you may not even need a plane to fly in from Miami Beach!

INGREDIENTS
- ¾ cup (180 ml) ketchup
- ½ cup (120 ml) pure maple syrup
- ¼ cup (60 ml) olive oil
- ¼ cup (60 ml) Jim Beam bourbon

- 2 tablespoons cider vinegar
- 2 tablespoons Dijon mustard

EQUIPMENT
Large mixing bowl

In a large mixing bowl, combine all the ingredients and stir for approximately 3 minutes, until the sauce is smooth and thick. Cover and refrigerate. Remove from the refrigerator early enough to serve at room temperature over barbecued, grilled, or broiled ribs, chicken, or beef. Makes 6 generous servings.

Did you know . . . ?

- Paul played the drums on "Back in the U.S.S.R." He apparently had driven Ringo crazy with his displeasure with Ringo's drumming; finally Ringo left the studio in a huff, saying he was quitting the band. Paul then sat in and re-recorded the drum part for the song. This is the version that appears on the *White Album.* (Ringo ultimately calmed down and returned to the band, remaining a Beatle until their final breakup.)

(Photo courtesy of Photofest)

Mother's Superior
Soups, Stews,
and Casseroles

Paella Lane

("Penny Lane")

One taste of this incredible chicken, sausage, and vegetable dish and you'll be singing, "Paella Lane is in my ears and in my eyes!" (Although to be accurate, you should probably change "ears" to "mouth," but then the alliteration would be lost.)

INGREDIENTS
1 pound (450 g) hot Italian sausage, cut into small pieces
¼ cup (70 ml) all-purpose flour
5 teaspoons salt
³/₈ teaspoon black pepper
4 pounds (1.8 kg) frying chicken parts
2 tablespoons olive oil
2 cups (550 ml) chopped onions
2 garlic cloves, minced
1 32-ounce (950 ml) can Italian tomatoes

2 cups (475 ml) water
1 tablespoon oregano
2 cups (550 ml) long-grain white rice
¼ teaspoon powdered saffron
1 pound (450 g) shrimp, shelled and deveined
1 cup (275 ml) mushrooms

EQUIPMENT
Large skillet
Large deep pot

Brown the sausage pieces in a skillet. Remove the browned sausage from the skillet and place in a large deep pot over medium heat.

Season the flour with 1 tablespoon of the salt and 1/8 teaspoon of the black pepper. Dredge the chicken parts in the seasoned flour. Add the olive oil to the sausage drippings in the skillet. Brown the chicken parts in the skillet. Remove the browned chicken parts from the skillet and add to the sausage in the pot.

Sauté the onions and garlic in the skillet. When the onions are soft, add the onions and garlic to the chicken and sausage in the pot. Add the tomatoes, water, oregano, and remaining salt and pepper to the pot. Simmer for 15 minutes. Stir in the rice and saffron and cook until the rice is tender (approximately 15 minutes). Add the shrimp and mushrooms. Cover and simmer for 15 to 20 minutes or until the shrimp is tender. Serves 10.

Lovely Linda's Vegetarian Feast

("Lovely Linda")

Linda McCartney—Paul's beloved wife of almost three decades—died on April 17, 1998, at the age of fifty-five, after a two-year battle with breast cancer. Linda was a passionate vegetarian and environmentalist and, with her husband, often spoke out against animal abuse, fur farms, animal testing, and other causes dear to her heart. Paul often told the story of when he and his wife became vegetarians: They were having leg of lamb for lunch one day and happened to glance out their kitchen window, where they saw one of their sheep grazing in a field. It suddenly struck them that they were all eating the *leg* of a *lamb.* That did it: They immediately swore off all meat. Linda even went on to create a vegetarian cookbook and a line of frozen vegetarian dinners.

Linda was committed to helping the world convert to a grain-based, fruit and vegetable diet. Her untimely death silenced her individual voice, but her compassion and passion touched millions. Her mission is being carried on by those who loved her—with her husband, Paul, as the most vocal (and most famous) spokesperson for her beliefs.

A classic shot of the McCartneys in the early days.
(Photo courtesy of Photofest)

The recipe for this delicious vegetable stew is respectfully dedicated to the memory of Linda McCartney. May we all remember (and help carry on) the wonderful work Linda did during her all-too-brief life.

INGREDIENTS
1¼ tablespoons olive oil
2 large red potatoes, cubed and boiled until firm-tender (approximately 15 to 20 minutes)
2 large onions, chopped
2 large mushrooms, chopped
1 10-ounce (285 g) package frozen peas, thawed

1 large tomato, cut up
8 ounces (235 ml) stewed tomatoes
Salt and black pepper to taste

EQUIPMENT
Large pot

Heat the olive oil in a large pot. Cook the potatoes and onions in the oil for 5 minutes. Add the mushrooms, peas, fresh tomato, and stewed tomatoes. Cook for 5 to 7 minutes more. Season with salt and pepper to taste. Serve with French bread and a good provolone cheese (if you don't mind eating dairy). Serves 4 to 6.

(Photo courtesy of Photofest)

Apple Corps Stew With Beef

(Apple Corps)

In February 1969, John Lennon wrote an untitled poem that had as its opening line, "A is for Parrot which we can plainly see." The last line of this "alphabet" poem read, "Z is for Apple which we can plainly see."

Unfortunately, the Beatles did *not* plainly see what was going on with Apple Corps' finances and management. When the company went broke, they seemed genuinely surprised.

This rich beef stew is dedicated to the ongoing legacy of Apple.

INGREDIENTS
- 2 tablespoons olive oil
- 1 pound (450 g) beef top round, cut into $1/2$- to 1-inch (13 to 25 mm) cubes
- 1 large onion, peeled and sliced
- 2 tablespoons all-purpose flour
- 2 tart apples, peeled, cored, and sliced
- 1 $13^{1}/_{4}$-ounce (392 ml) can beef broth
- $1/2$ teaspoon dried sage
- 1 large potato, peeled and cubed
- 1 cup (275 ml) frozen peas and carrots, thawed

EQUIPMENT
Large pot

In a large pot, heat the olive oil and brown the beef on all sides. Stir in the onion and cook over a medium flame until the onion is soft. Stir in the flour, apple slices, beef broth, and sage. Heat to a boil, reduce the heat, cover, and simmer for $1^{1}/_{2}$ hours or until the beef is tender. Add the cubed potatoes and simmer for another 20 minutes. Stir in the peas and carrots and simmer until they're cooked. Serve hot with a tossed salad and garlic bread. Serves 4 (or 2 big eaters!).

Got to Get Ratatouille Into My Life

("Got to Get You Into My Life")

This baked vegetable casserole is a delight that you'll want to keep in your life for a good long time.

INGREDIENTS
- 2 cups (550 ml) peeled and cubed eggplant
- 1 teaspoon garlic powder
- $1/2$ cup (120 ml) olive oil
- $1^1/_2$ teaspoons salt
- 2 cups (550 ml) finely chopped onions
- 2 tablespoons dry white wine
- 1 cup (275 ml) red pepper strips
- 1 cup (275 ml) green pepper strips
- 2 cups (550 ml) fresh tomato slices
- $1/2$ teaspoon oregano
- $1/8$ teaspoon black pepper
- $1/2$ cup (140 ml) shredded Swiss cheese

EQUIPMENT
$2^1/_2$-quart (2.4 l) casserole dish
Aluminum foil

Preheat the oven to 350° F (177° C). Spread the eggplant over the bottom of the casserole dish. Sprinkle the eggplant with 1/3 teaspoon of the garlic powder, 2 tablespoons of the olive oil, and 1/2 teaspoon of the salt. Top the eggplant with the onions. On top of the onions, sprinkle 1/2 teaspoon of garlic powder, 2 tablespoons of olive oil, the white wine, and 1/2 teaspoon of salt. Top with a layer of red peppers and a layer of green peppers. Sprinkle the peppers with the remaining olive oil, garlic powder, pepper, and salt. Cover with aluminum foil and bake for 45 minutes.

Uncover and lay the tomato slices on top of the vegetables. Baste the tomatoes with some of the juice from the pan, and sprinkle with oregano. Top the casserole with the shredded Swiss cheese. Bake uncovered for 15 more minutes. Serve with crusty bread and grated cheese.

Did you know . . . ?

🍎 During their 1966 U.S. tour, the Beatles had reached a level of fame unprecedented in pop-culture history. John once recalled mothers actually bringing blind kids into the Beatles' dressing room and begging any of the band members to just kiss the children. The mothers believed that John, Paul, George, or Ringo's "holy touch" would miraculously bring back their child's sight.

Things We Stewed Today

("Things We Said Today")

This delicious and hearty beef stew will surely have you singing, "Me, I'm just the lucky kind!" as you reminisce about "things we stewed today."

INGREDIENTS

3 *tablespoons olive oil*

2 *pounds (900 g) stewing beef, cut into bite-sized pieces*

2 *tablespoons all-purpose flour*

1 *teaspoon salt*

¼ *teaspoon black pepper*

¼ *teaspoon dried thyme*

1 *cup (235 ml) red wine*

1 *3-ounce (90 g) can sliced mushrooms*

4 *carrots, cut into strips*

1 *4-ounce (115 g) jar white onions*

1 *16-ounce (450 g) can round white potatoes*

1 *cup (235 ml) beef broth*

EQUIPMENT

Large skillet

3-quart (2.85 l) casserole baking dish

Mixing bowl

Preheat the oven to 325° F (163° C). Heat the olive oil in a large skillet. Brown the beef on all sides in the olive oil. When the meat is browned, stir in the flour, salt, pepper, and thyme. Mix well. Transfer the contents of the skillet to the casserole baking dish. In a bowl, mix together the red wine and the beef broth; pour it over the meat. Cover the casserole and bake for 2¹/₂ hours. Add the mushrooms, carrots, onions, and potatoes. Stir together, cover, and bake for 35 minutes more, or until the carrots are tender. Serve with garlic bread. Serves 6 to 8.

Gumboot Gumbo With Shrimp

("Come Together")

You will be delighted at the way the different ingredients in this classic New Orleans–inspired gumbo all "come together" with such wonderful results!

INGREDIENTS

- 1 16-ounce (450 g) package frozen cut okra, thawed
- 3 large onions, sliced
- 1 16-ounce (475 ml) can stewed tomatoes
- 2 cups (475 ml) water
- ¹/₂ pound (225 g) dry hot sausage, sliced
- 1 8-ounce (235 ml) can tomato sauce
- 2 tablespoons (¹/₄ stick) salted butter
- 2 garlic cloves, chopped
- ¹/₂ teaspoon crushed red pepper flakes
- 1 bay leaf
- 2 pounds (900 g) medium shrimp, shelled and deveined

EQUIPMENT
Large heavy kettle with cover

Combine the okra, onions, stewed tomatoes, water, hot sausage, tomato sauce, butter, garlic, red pepper flakes, and bay leaf in a large kettle and heat to boiling. Reduce the heat and simmer partially covered for 30 minutes. Add the shrimp to the kettle and mix well. Cook, partially covered, for 10 to 15 minutes more, stirring occasionally, until shrimp is cooked through. Serves 6.

With a Little Help From My Frankfurters

("With a Little Help From My Friends")

Would you believe in a love at first taste? You will with your first fork-ful of this delicious casserole! I'm certain that it happens all the time.

INGREDIENTS

2 tablespoons chopped onion

2 tablespoons chopped green pepper

2 tablespoons (¹/₄ stick) salted butter

6 frankfurters, cut into bite-sized pieces

¹/₄ teaspoon celery salt

Black pepper to taste

¹/₂ cup (120 ml) milk

1 10¹/₂-ounce (310 ml) can condensed cheddar cheese soup

2 cups (550 ml) cooked noodles (approximately 4 ounces/ 115 g uncooked noodles)

³/₄ cup (210 ml) grated Parmesan cheese

EQUIPMENT

Skillet

Casserole baking dish

Preheat the oven to 350° F (177° C). Heat the butter in a skillet. Sauté the onion and green pepper in the butter until the onion is soft. Add the cut-up frankfurters, celery salt, and black pepper to taste. Stir. Add the milk and can of cheddar cheese soup and mix well. Pour the contents of the skillet into a casserole dish. Add the cooked noodles and mix well. Sprinkle the top of the casserole with grated Parmesan. Cover and bake for 30 minutes. Serve with a garden salad and French bread. Serves 6.

Did you know . . . ?

● In 1970 then U.S. Vice President Spiro Agnew lobbied for an American radio ban of the Beatles song "With a Little Help From My Friends" because of its line about getting "high with a little help from my friends." Agnew also wanted a ban imposed on "Lucy in the Sky With Diamonds" because of the alleged (yet spurious) reference to LSD in its title.

Inside a Zoo-Chini Stew

("Baby, You're a Rich Man")

In "Baby, You're a Rich Man," John sings about a rich man keeping all his money in a "big brown bag, inside a zoo. What a thing to do." I agree, and feel that zucchini stew is a much better thing to keep in a bag in a zoo: This way, if you get hungry, you're all set! (But I recommend a plastic Ziploc bag.)

INGREDIENTS
Nonstick vegetable cooking spray
2 *medium zucchini, cubed*
2 *medium potatoes, cubed*
1 *large onion, chopped*
1 *8-ounce (235 ml) can tomato sauce*

Salt and black pepper to taste

EQUIPMENT
Large glass casserole baking dish
Aluminum foil

Preheat the oven to 350° F (177° C). Spray a large glass casserole baking dish with vegetable cooking spray. Place the zucchini, potatoes, onion, and tomato sauce in the casserole and mix well. Add salt and pepper to taste. Cover the casserole with aluminum foil and bake for 30 minutes, until the potatoes are cooked. Serve as a vegetarian main dish or a vegetable side dish. Serves 4.

Did you know . . . ?

🍎 In September 1995 Paul McCartney's handwritten lyrics for the *Sgt. Pepper* song "Getting Better" sold at auction for $250,902.

Eleanor Rigby's Rice and Spinach Soup

("Eleanor Rigby")

Eleanor Rigby might have made this delicious soup with the rice she picked up in a church where a wedding had been . . . but you can buy the rice—and all your other ingredients—at your favorite grocery store.

INGREDIENTS
- 1 10-ounce (285 g) package frozen chopped spinach
- 6 cups (1.4 l) beef broth
- 2 tablespoons (¹/₄ stick) salted butter
- ¹/₂ teaspoon salt
- ¹/₂ cup (140 ml) Minute Rice
- ¹/₄ cup (70 ml) grated Parmesan cheese

EQUIPMENT
Large saucepan

Combine the spinach, beef broth, butter, and salt in a large saucepan and bring to a boil. Simmer for 10 minutes. Add the Minute Rice and cook for 5 minutes more. Sprinkle with grated Parmesan before serving. Serves 6.

Did you know . . . ?

- 🍎 Originally, the character of Father McKenzie in "Eleanor Rigby" was named Father McCartney. Paul realized that people would think he was referring to his own father and decided he didn't want his dad associated with such a lonely song, so he looked through a phone book and found the name McKenzie, which he used instead. In September 1980 John Lennon told *Playboy* magazine that he always thought that "Father McCartney" sounded better than "McKenzie."

Veal Love

("Real Love")

Even though John Lennon had embraced macrobiotic vegetarianism at varying times during his life, at the time of his death he seems to have gone back to eating meat. There are reports of his taste for Japanese Kobe beef and his occasional indulgence in bacon and other carnivorous delights. Thus, this recipe is dedicated to John in his final years, when the odds are he would have enjoyed a dish of this delicious stew—even though he would have probably felt a little guilty about it after he ate it!

INGREDIENTS
1/2 cup (120 ml) olive oil
3 pounds (1.4 kg) stew veal,
    cut into bite-sized pieces
2 1/2 cups (595 ml) dry white wine
1 1/2 teaspoons garlic powder
1/2 teaspoon black pepper
1/2 teaspoon salt
1 8-ounce (225 g) can sliced
    mushrooms, drained

1 medium onion, chopped
1 16-ounce (450 g) can round
    white potatoes, drained
1 1/2 cups (355 ml) water

EQUIPMENT
Large skillet

In a large skillet, heat the olive oil. Add the stew veal, wine, garlic powder, black pepper, and salt to the skillet and cook for 15 minutes, stirring often. Add the mushrooms, onion, potatoes, and water to the skillet. Cover and simmer for 1 to 2 hours, stirring often, until the veal is tender. For the last 10 minutes of cooking, lower the heat and allow some of the liquid in the skillet to evaporate. Serve with Italian or French bread. Serves 4 to 6.

Did you know . . . ?

● According to the Recording Industry Association of America (RIAA), the Beatles have the most certified gold disks of any group. Their total of sixty gold disks includes thirty-eight albums and twenty-two singles.

It's Minestrone Love

("It's Only Love")

Just one taste of this scrumptious main-dish Italian soup will have you singing, "Just the sight of you makes nighttime bright." (*Very* bright!)

INGREDIENTS
- 1 tablespoon olive oil
- 2 ounces (60 g) salt pork, diced
- 2 garlic cloves, minced
- 1 small onion, chopped
- 1 teaspoon chopped fresh basil
- 1 teaspoon parsley
- 2 celery stalks, chopped
- 2 cups (475 ml) canned Italian crushed tomatoes
- 2 carrots, chopped
- 2 small heads cabbage, chopped

- 6 cups (1.425 l) cold water
  Salt and black pepper to taste
- 4 ounces (115 g) canned white cannelloni beans
- 4 ounces (115 g) canned red kidney beans
- 1 cup (275 ml) uncooked ditalini pasta (tubetti)
  Grated Romano cheese

EQUIPMENT
Large soup kettle

Rushing home for a piping hot bowl of It's Minestrone Love.
(Photo courtesy of Photofest)

In a large soup kettle, heat the olive oil. Add the salt pork, garlic, onion, basil, and parsley and cook until the salt pork is lightly browned. Add the celery, crushed tomatoes, carrots, cabbage, and cold water, and bring to a slow boil. Taste and season with salt and black pepper as needed. Cover the kettle and cook for 45 to 50 minutes, until the celery and carrots are tender. Add the white and red beans and ditalini pasta to the kettle and cook for 10 minutes more. Serve with grated Romano cheese and Italian bread. Serves 6 to 8.

Did you know . . . ?

🍎 John once admitted that of all the songs he wrote for the Beatles, the only one he absolutely hated was "It's Only Love." "Terrible lyric," he told *Hit Parader* magazine in 1972.

This Boy's
Beef, Pork, and
Veal Dishes

Liver or Let Die

("Live or Let Die")

This delicious dish is what James Bond was really chasing after in *Live or Let Die*! (Honest.)

INGREDIENTS
1½ *pounds (675 g) calf's liver*
 ½ *pound (225 g) bacon*
 8 *large onions*
   Salt and black pepper to taste

EQUIPMENT
Large heavy skillet
Pastry brush

Cut the liver into small pieces. Cut the bacon into small pieces. Slice the onions. Cook the bacon in a large heavy skillet with the onions until the bacon is cooked. Add the liver, salt, and pepper. Cook slowly for 30 minutes. Serves 8.

Did you know . . . ?

🍎 Paul McCartney adapted the lyrics for *Abbey Road*'s lovely ballad "Golden Slumbers" from a four-hundred-year-old poem of the same name by Thomas Decker, which he came across one day at his father's house.

I Want to Hold Your Ham (Pie)

("I Want to Hold Your Hand")

This rich Italian Easter specialty will make you want to do more than hold the cook's hand, that's for sure!

INGREDIENTS

CRUST

2¹/₂ cups (690 ml) all-purpose
    flour
¹/₂ teaspoon salt
¹/₂ cup (140 ml) vegetable
    shortening
1 medium egg
    Water (as needed for a
    spreadable consistency)

FILLING

8 medium eggs
¹/₂ pound (225 g) ricotta cheese

¹/₂ pound (225 g) prosciutto,
    diced small
¹/₂ pound (225 g) dried
    Abruzzesse sausage, diced
    small
¹/₂ pound (225 g) fresh farmer's
    cheese

EQUIPMENT

Large mixing bowl
10 inch round × 3 inch deep
    (25 × 8 cm) baking pan

Sift together the flour and salt, and add the shortening with a fork. Mix well, then add the egg along with enough water to make the consistency of the dough spreadable. Refrigerate for 10 minutes.

Roll the dough out 1/8 inch (3 mm) thick and fit into greased and floured baking pan. Reserve enough dough to cover the top of the pan.

Preheat the oven to 450° F (232° C). Beat the eggs with the ricotta cheese. Add the prosciutto, sausage, and farmer's cheese, and mix well. Spoon the filling into the dough-lined baking pan. Cover the top with the remainder of the dough and flute the edges of the crust. Bake for 30 minutes. Reduce the heat to 375° F (190° C) and bake for 45 minutes more. Remove from the oven and let the pie cool in its pan for at least 1 hour before removing it. Serves 20.

I've Just Stuffed a Steak

("I've Just Seen a Face")

Everybody sing along: I've just stuffed a steak, I can't forget the time or place, Where we just et, It was the beef for me, And I want all the world to see we're fed! Mmm, mmm, mmm, mmm, mmm, mmm!

INGREDIENTS
  2 pounds (900 g) flank steak
 ½ cup (140 ml) chopped onion
  1 garlic clove
  1 teaspoon olive oil

STUFFING
  1 slightly beaten medium egg
  1 10-ounce (285 g) package
     frozen spinach, cooked and
     drained
 ½ cup (140 ml) shredded
     shrimp
 ¼ cup (60 ml) cold water
  2 ounces (60 g) provolone
     cheese
 ¼ teaspoon dried sage
 ¼ teaspoon garlic powder
 ¼ teaspoon salt
     Dash black pepper

 ¾ cup (210 ml) soft bread
     crumbs

GRAVY
 ½ cup (120 ml) dry red wine
  1 8-ounce (235 ml) can tomato
     sauce
  2 tablespoons all-purpose flour

EQUIPMENT
Meat pounder
Large mixing bowl
Wooden spatula
Large skillet
String
10 × 12 inch (25 × 30 cm)
    baking dish
Small mixing bowl
Aluminum foil

Preheat the oven to 350° F (177° C). Pound the flank steak until it is approximately 1¼ inches (3 cm) thick and set it aside.

To make the stuffing, combine the egg, spinach, shrimp, cold water, provolone, sage, garlic powder, salt, pepper, and bread crumbs in a large bowl. Mix well. Using a wooden spatula, spread the stuffing mixture onto the steak.

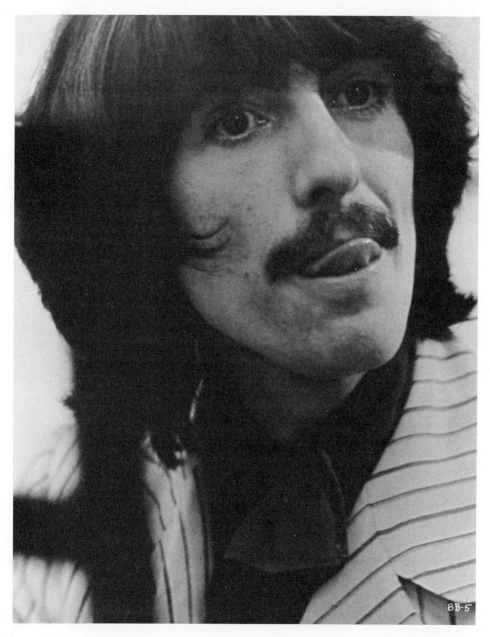

"Mmm, Mmm! Love that Let It Beef." (Photo courtesy of Photofest)

In a skillet, brown the chopped onion and garlic clove in the olive oil. Remove the onion and garlic from the skillet and spread them on top of the stuffing mixture on the steak. Roll the steak into a tube and tie it with the string. Brown the steak on both sides in the skillet that you used to cook the onion and garlic.

Remove the steak from the skillet and place it in the baking dish. Combine the tomato sauce and wine in a small mixing bowl and pour over the steak. Cover the baking dish with aluminum foil and bake for $1^1/_2$ hours.

Remove the steak from the baking dish and make a gravy by adding the flour to the steak's pan juices and mixing until it is a smooth consistency. Pour the gravy over the stuffed steak and serve with garlic bread, a tossed green salad, and a vegetable of your choice. (Baked potatoes or string beans are especially good.) Serves 6 to 8.

Let It Beef

("Let It Be")

"Let It Be" was inspired by a dream Paul had of his mother. This stroganoff recipe is in honor of "Mother Mary" and her powerful influence on her son and his music.

INGREDIENTS
1 pound (450 g) sirloin, $^1/_4$ inch (6 mm) thick
1 garlic clove, peeled
3 tablespoons all-purpose flour
$1^3/_4$ teaspoons salt
$^1/_4$ teaspoon pepper
$^1/_4$ teaspoon paprika
$^1/_4$ cup (70 ml) vegetable shortening
$^1/_3$ cup (90 ml) chopped onion

$1^3/_4$ cups (415 ml) beef bouillon
1 pound (450 g) fresh mushrooms, sliced
$^1/_2$ cup (120 ml) sour cream
2 tablespoons fresh chives, cut fine

EQUIPMENT
Large mixing bowl
Large heavy skillet

Rub both sides of the sirloin with the garlic, then cut the meat into 1¹/₂ × 1 inch (38 × 25 mm) strips. In a large bowl, mix the flour, salt, pepper, and paprika. Add the sirloin strips a few at a time, tossing them until they are well coated with the seasoned flour. Reserve the remaining seasoned flour. Heat the vegetable shortening in a heavy skillet. Add the sirloin strips and brown well on all sides. Add the onion to the skillet and continue cooking until transparent. Add the remaining seasoned flour, bouillon, and mushrooms to the skillet. Cover and cook slowly for about 1¹/₂ hours, stirring occasionally, until the meat is tender. Remove the cover and continue cooking until the sauce begins to thicken slightly. Add the sour cream and chives and blend well. Serve over fettuccine or ziti. Serves 4.

She's Leaving Bones

("She's Leaving Home")

Money can buy pork ribs and barbecue sauce, and since eating these messy morsels sure is a lot of fun, I guess Mr. McCartney was confused when he sang in "She's Leaving Home" that "fun is the one thing that money can't buy," eh?

INGREDIENTS

3 pounds (1.4 kg) country-style pork ribs

BARBECUE SAUCE

1 tablespoon corn oil
1 cup (275 ml) chopped onion
1 garlic clove, minced
8 ounces (235 ml) tomato sauce
¹/₄ cup (70 ml) packed brown sugar

3 tablespoons lemon juice
2 tablespoons Worcestershire sauce
1 tablespoon prepared mustard
¹/₂ teaspoon celery seeds
¹/₂ cup (120 ml) water
¹/₄ teaspoon black pepper

EQUIPMENT
Roasting pan
Medium saucepan

Preheat the oven to 350° F (177° C). Bake the ribs on a rack in a roasting pan for 1 hour. While the ribs are roasting, prepare the barbecue sauce: Heat the corn oil in a medium saucepan until it is hot, and in it cook the onion and garlic until soft. Stir in the tomato sauce, brown sugar, lemon juice, Worcestershire sauce, mustard, celery seeds, water, and teaspoon pepper. Simmer the sauce for 15 minutes, stirring occasionally. Drain the grease from the bottom of the roasting pan and generously spoon the barbecue sauce over the ribs. Cover the pan and roast the ribs for another 30 to 60 minutes, depending on how well done you like them. Occasionally baste the ribs with the sauce as they are cooking. Serve with a tossed salad, corn on the cob, and *lots* of napkins. Serves 4.

I Veal Fine

("I Feel Fine")

This rich and flavorful (and truly unique!) veal dish will guarantee that your dinner guests will leave your table "as happy as can be"!

INGREDIENTS

- 4 *large veal cutlets, pounded flat*
  Salt and black pepper
- 2 *tablespoons all-purpose flour*
- 1 *tablespoon salted butter*
- 1 *tablespoon olive oil*
  Nonstick vegetable cooking spray
- 2 *tablespoons anchovies, mashed into a spreadable pulp*
- 4 *slices fresh tomato*
- 2 *teaspoons oregano*
- 4 *1-ounce (30 g) slices mozzarella cheese*
- 4 *large black olives, pitted*
- 1 *tablespoon chopped fresh basil*

EQUIPMENT
Large skillet
Flat broiler pan

Season the veal cutlets with salt and pepper and dredge each cutlet in the flour. Heat the butter and olive oil in a skillet until the butter is melted. Fry the veal cutlets in the skillet until they are brown on both sides. Spray a flat broiler pan lightly with nonstick vegetable cooking spray. Transfer the veal cutlets from the skillet to the broiler pan. Turn on the oven's top broiler. Spread a thin layer of the mashed anchovy pulp on each cutlet. Place a tomato slice on top of each cutlet. Sprinkle each tomato slice with oregano. Place a slice of mozzarella on top of each tomato slice. Place a large black olive on top of each cutlet.

Place the cutlets under the broiler and heat until the mozzarella begins to melt. Remove from the oven and sprinkle each cutlet with chopped basil. Serve immediately with a tossed salad, mashed potatoes, and plain dinner rolls. Serves 4.

Did you know . . . ?

🍎 The feedback beginning of "I Feel Fine" was the first time feedback was ever used on a recording. The feedback was accidental, but the Fabs liked the way it sounded so they left it in.

"Roll Up" Meat Loaf

("Magical Mystery Tour")

You won't need to "make a reservation" when you make this delectable meat loaf roll-up at home!

INGREDIENTS

1½ pounds (675 g) lean ground beef
1 medium egg
½ cup (140 ml) Italian-seasoned bread crumbs
¼ cup (70 ml) unsalted soda cracker crumbs
½ cup (140 ml) finely chopped onion
2 8-ounce (235 ml each) cans tomato sauce
4 ounces (115 g) grated Parmesan cheese
1 teaspoon salt
½ teaspoon oregano

¹/₈ teaspoon black pepper
2 cups (550 ml) shredded
   mozzarella cheese
   Nonstick vegetable cooking
   spray

EQUIPMENT
Large mixing bowl
Wax paper
10 × 12 inch (25 × 30 cm) baking
   dish

Preheat the oven to 350° F (177° C). In a large mixing bowl, combine the ground beef, egg, bread crumbs, cracker crumbs, onion, 1/3 cup (75 ml) of the tomato sauce, grated Parmesan, salt, oregano, and black pepper, and mix well. On a sheet of wax paper, shape the meat mixture into a loaf 10 × 12 inches (25 × 30 cm) in size. Sprinkle the shredded mozzarella evenly on top of the meat. Carefully roll up the meat like a jelly roll and press the ends closed to seal. Spray the baking dish with vegetable cooking spray. Lift the meat loaf off the wax paper and transfer it to the baking dish. Bake for 1 hour. Drain off any accumulated fat from the pan and pour the remainder of the tomato sauce on and around the meat loaf. Bake for 15 minutes more. Let stand a few minutes before slicing. Serve with a garden salad, buttered white rice, and a crusty bread. Serves 6 to 8.

Did you know . . . ?

● On March 22, 1997, Julian Lennon paid $55,998 for the afghan coat worn by his father on the cover of the 1967 *Magical Mystery Tour* album.

Watching the Veal

("Watching the Wheels")

Was John thinking of this delicious veal Parmesan recipe when he wrote his wonderful *Double Fantasy* song, "Watching the Wheels"? After all, if he was sitting in his Dakota Arms kitchen "watching the veal" cook one afternoon, it's not that much of a stretch to imagine the Artist Lennon playing with the words and coming up with one of his most memorable songs, now is it? Just a thought.

INGREDIENTS

1½ pounds (675 g) veal cutlets, cut from the leg
1 cup (275 ml) Italian-seasoned bread crumbs
¼ cup (70 ml) grated Parmesan cheese
1 garlic clove, minced
½ teaspoon salt
⅛ teaspoon black pepper
⅛ teaspoon oregano
½ cup (120 ml) olive oil
2 medium eggs, beaten
Olive-oil-flavored nonstick vegetable cooking spray
1 cup (235 ml) tomato sauce (fresh or jarred)
¾ cup (210 ml) shredded mozzarella cheese

EQUIPMENT

2 mixing bowls for dipping
Large skillet
Large baking dish

Cut the veal into 3 × 3 inch (7.5 × 7.5 cm) pieces. In a mixing bowl, combine the bread crumbs, most of the grated Parmesan cheese (reserve some to sprinkle on cutlets before baking), garlic, salt, pepper, and oregano. Mix well. Heat the olive oil in the skillet. Dip each cutlet into the beaten egg and then coat well with the bread crumb mixture. Fry each cutlet in the skillet until golden brown on both sides. Preheat the oven to 375° F (190° C). Spray a baking dish with olive-oil-flavored vegetable cooking spray. Arrange the veal cutlets in the dish. Spoon tomato sauce on top of the cutlets. Sprinkle the cutlets with the remaining grated Parmesan cheese and cover with the shredded mozzarella. Bake for 15 minutes, or until the cheese melts. Serve immediately with a tossed salad and garlic bread. Serves 4.

A very young John, many years before Watching the Veal.
(Photo courtesy of Photofest; photo by Astrid Kirchherr)

Chuck's Chuck Roast

("When I'm Sixty-Four")

Vera and Dave insisted that I tell you that they helped with this recipe.

INGREDIENTS
  3-pound (1.4 kg) chuck roast,
    2 inches (5 cm) thick
  2 tablespoons A-1 Steak Sauce
  1 envelope onion soup mix
  1 10^1/$_2$-ounce (310 ml) can
    condensed cream of
    mushroom soup

EQUIPMENT
  Aluminum foil
  Large roasting pan

Preheat the oven to 350° F (177° C). Place the roast on an oversized piece of aluminum foil. Brush the meat with the A-1 Steak Sauce. Sprinkle the envelope of onion soup mix on the meat, then spoon the mushroom soup onto it. (The soup will be thick. Use the back of the spoon to spread it evenly over the roast.) Pull up the side of the aluminum foil and wrap the roast, sealing it securely. Place the foil-wrapped roast in a large roasting pan and bake for 2^1/$_2$ to 3 hours. Allow it to stand for a few minutes before slicing. Serve with baked potatoes, string beans, and garlic bread. Serves 4 to 6.

Did you know . . . ?

🍎 In 1967 Paul McCartney's father, Jim McCartney, turned sixty-four. In honor of his birthday, Paul resurrected a song he (Paul) had written when he was in his teens—"When I'm Sixty-Four"—revised and improved it, and ultimately decided to include the tune on the *Sgt. Pepper* album.

Plasticine Pork Chops With Chopped Thyme and Rice

("Lucy in the Sky With Diamonds")

Recipe title notwithstanding, you can buy *regular* pork chops for this delicious dish.

INGREDIENTS
- 4 thick pork chops (bone-in)
  Salt and black pepper
- 1 tablespoon salted butter
- 2 tablespoons olive oil
- 3/4 cup (210 ml) long-grain rice
- 4 ounces (140 ml) thinly-sliced baked ham
- 1 garlic clove, sliced
- 1 tablespoon parsley
- 1/4 teaspoon dried thyme
- 1/2 cup (120 ml) dry white wine
- 1 cup (235 ml) chicken bouillon
- 1 cup (275 ml) thin-sliced onion
- 1/2 cup (140 ml) thin-sliced celery
- 1/2 cup (140 ml) thin-sliced green pepper
- 1/2 cup (140 ml) thin-sliced mushrooms

EQUIPMENT
10-inch (25 cm) skillet

Trim the fat from the pork chops and season them on both sides with salt and pepper. Heat the butter and olive oil in the skillet. Place the chops in the skillet and slowly brown them on both sides. Remove from the skillet and set aside. Place the long-grain rice in the skillet and stir it in the oil and butter for 2 minutes. Return the pork chops to the skillet. Cover the chops with the baked ham, garlic, parsley, and thyme. Add the wine to the skillet and simmer for 2 minutes. Add the chicken bouillon to the skillet and cover the pan tightly. Simmer for 30 minutes, until the pork is thoroughly cooked. Add the onion, celery, green pepper, and mushrooms to the skillet and simmer for another 8 to 10 minutes, until the vegetables are cooked but still crisp. Serves 4.

Let Me Roast It
("Let Me Roll It")

Your taste buds will take "Wings" when you first try this delicious pork roast entrée. (Appropriately, Paul and Wings' *Band on the Run* album makes wonderful background "dining music" for this enticing dish.)

INGREDIENTS

1 envelope Lipton Onion Soup mix

²/₃ cup (155 ml) water

²/₃ cup (155 ml) honey

¹/₄ cup (60 ml) ketchup

2 tablespoons lemon juice

2 teaspoons grated lemon rind

1 cup (275 ml) pitted mixed dried fruit

4-pound (1.8 kg) pork roast

EQUIPMENT

Medium mixing bowl

Large casserole baking dish

Aluminum foil

Preheat the oven to 325° F (163° C). In a medium mixing bowl, combine the onion soup mix, water, honey, ketchup, lemon juice, lemon rind, and half of the mixed fruit. Mix well. Cut deep slits in the pork roast between the chops, and insert the remaining fruit pieces into these slits. Place the pork roast in a large baking dish. Pour the fruited soup mix over it. Cover the pan with aluminum foil and bake for 1¹/₂ to 2 hours. Uncover the roast and bake for an additional 45 minutes or until the it's cooked the way you like it. Let it stand for a few minutes before carving. Serve with a garden salad and yams. Serves 6.

He Shoot Coca-Cola Pork Chops

("Come Together")

The reason old flattop is grooving up slowly? He wants to savor every bite of these wonderfully different baked pork chops!

INGREDIENTS	EQUIPMENT
8 thick pork chops	Large casserole baking dish
Salt and black pepper to taste	Mixing bowl
1 cup (235 ml) ketchup	
1 cup (235 ml) Coca-Cola	
Brown sugar to taste	

Preheat the oven to 350° F (177° C). Place the pork chops in a casserole baking dish and sprinkle on both sides with salt and pepper to taste. In a mixing bowl, combine the ketchup and Coca-Cola. Mix well. Pour the sauce over the pork chops, then sprinkle the chops with brown sugar to taste. Bake uncovered for 1 hour (or until the chops are done the way you like them). Serve with buttered broccoli and candied yams. Serves 6 to 8.

Did you know . . . ?

- The Beatles' *Abbey Road* single "Come Together" was initially banned from being played on the BBC because of the reference to Coca-Cola in its lyrics. The BBC considered any mention of a brand name in a pop song to be advertising, and thus refused to air it.

Norwegian Wood-Smoked Ribs

("Norwegian Wood [This Bird Has Flown]")

Did you know that the original opening line of "Norwegian Wood" was "I once had a grill"? Really.

INGREDIENTS

MEAT

  4 *pounds (1.8 kg) meaty pork spareribs*

WOOD CHIPS

  4 *cups (1.1 l) hickory wood chips*

SEASONING RUB

  1 *tablespoon brown sugar*
  1 *teaspoon 5-spice seasoning powder*
$^1/_2$ *teaspoon paprika*
$^1/_4$ *teaspoon salt*

$^1/_4$ *teaspoon celery seeds*
$^1/_4$ *teaspoon black pepper*

RIB GLAZE

$^1/_2$ *cup (120 ml) ketchup*
  2 *tablespoons light molasses*
  1 *tablespoon lemon juice*
  1 *tablespoon soy sauce*
   Several dashes hot pepper sauce (bottled)

EQUIPMENT

Large covered kettle
Mixing bowl
Barbecue grill with drip pan

Prepare the ribs: Cut the ribs into individual-serving-sized pieces. Place in a large kettle and add enough water to cover them completely. Bring the pot to a boil and then reduce the heat. Cover the kettle and simmer the ribs for 30 minutes. Thoroughly drain the ribs and allow them to cool.

  Prepare the hickory wood chips: Soak the wood chips for at least 1 hour in enough water to cover them completely. Thoroughly drain the chips before using.

  Prepare the seasoning rub: In a mixing bowl, combine the brown sugar, 5-spice powder, paprika, salt, celery seeds, and pepper. Mix well. When the cooked ribs are cool enough to handle, rub them all over with the seasoning rub on both sides.

Make the rib glaze: In a mixing bowl, combine the ketchup, molasses, lemon juice, and soy sauce. Mix well. Squirt several dashes of bottled hot pepper sauce (more or less to taste) into the bowl and mix well. Set aside.

Prepare the barbecue grill: Light the coals and allow them to heat to medium cooking temperature. When the coals are hot, arrange them around a good-sized drip pan in a covered grill. Sprinkle the drained hickory chips evenly onto the hot coals.

Barbecue the ribs: Place a grill rack above the drip pan and put the precooked ribs on the rack. Cover the grill and cook the ribs for at least 45 to 50 minutes, or until they are tender and no pink remains inside. During the last 15 minutes of cooking, frequently brush the ribs generously with the spicy glaze. Serve with a green salad, corn on the cob, baked potatoes, and garlic bread. Serves 4.

Ringo performs his version of The Chicken Dance, as he waits for a place at the table. (Photo courtesy of Photofest)

"Come Together"
Chicken and Turkey
Main Dishes

And Your Breasts Can Sing

("And Your Bird Can Sing")

John once said that he considered his song "And Your Bird Can Sing" a "horror" and a "throwaway." I tell you this so that I can now apologize for this horrible segue into a truly delicious recipe: You sure as heck won't want to "throw away" these stuffed chicken breasts! (See? I told you.)

INGREDIENTS
4 large boneless chicken
   breasts

STUFFING
1 loaf day-old Italian
   bread
2 medium eggs
$^1/_4$ cup (70 ml) grated Parmesan
   cheese
2 tablespoons parsley
10 black olives, chopped
   Salt and black pepper to
   taste
$^1/_2$ onion, chopped

2 ounces (60 g) pepperoni,
   cut into small cubes (stick
   pepperoni works best; if
   not available, use sliced
   pepperoni and cut into
   small pieces)
$^1/_4$ cup ($^1/_2$ stick) salted butter
1 10$^1/_2$-ounce (310 ml) can
   condensed cream of
   chicken soup
$^1/_4$ cup (60 ml) white wine

EQUIPMENT
Large mixing bowl
Large deep skillet
12 toothpicks

113

Place the loaf of hard Italian bread in a bowl of water and soak until it is soft. Squeeze out the excess water, discard the water from the bowl, and place the bread back into the empty bowl. To the soaked bread, add the eggs, grated Parmesan, parsley, black olives, and salt and pepper to taste. Mix well.

In a large skillet, sauté the chopped onion and pepperoni cubes in the butter. When the onion is soft, spoon the mix over the bread stuffing mixture, leaving the butter in the skillet. Add extra bread crumbs to the stuffing mixture if needed to create a firm consistency. Mix well. Place an equal amount of stuffing on each chicken breast. Roll them up and use 3 toothpicks to hold each breast together.

Place the stuffed chicken breasts in the skillet and brown each side for 15 minutes. Add the chicken soup and white wine to the skillet. Simmer the breasts slowly for 20 more minutes, until done. Do not overcook. Serve with a tossed green salad and baked or mashed potatoes. Serves 4.

Did you know . . . ?

🍎 In "The Continuing Story of Bungalow Bill" on the *White Album,* Yoko Ono sings the line, "Not when he looked so fierce." This was the first time a female had ever sung on a Beatles record. (It was also Yoko's singing debut on record.)

(Photo Courtesy of Photofest)

She Legs You

("She Loves You")

This really delicious baked chicken recipe will have you (and your dinner companions) shouting, "Yeah, yeah, *yeah!*" (Contributed by Lee Mandato.)

INGREDIENTS

6 whole skinless chicken legs
   *(drumstick and thigh
   attached)*
1 *16-ounce (475 ml) bottle
   Italian salad dressing (oil-
   and-vinegar based, not
   creamy)
   Paprika*

EQUIPMENT

*10 × 13 inch (25 × 33 cm) baking
   dish*

Wash the chicken legs in cold water and pat dry. Preheat the oven to 350° F (177° C). Arrange the legs in the baking dish, pour 8 ounces (235 ml) of the salad dressing over them, and sprinkle generously with paprika. Bake for 30 to 40 minutes, until the tops of the legs are brown. Turn the legs over and pour the remaining salad dressing over them. Sprinkle again with paprika and bake for 30 more minutes. Serve with a tossed salad and baked potatoes, or with chopped broccoli drizzled with a little of the salad dressing, and buttered white rice. Serves 4 to 6.

Did you know . . . ?

● When Paul McCartney's father first heard "She Loves You" with its "Yeah, yeah, yeah" chorus, he suggested they change it to "Yes, yes, yes," because it was more "dignified." Thankfully, the senior McCartney's suggestion was not acted upon.

I Should Have Flown Better
("I Should Have Known Better")

"I Should Have Known Better"—the B side of the "Hard Day's Night" single—was performed in the film *A Hard Day's Night*. The Fabs sang it in a train baggage compartment as a few lovely lasses looked on. The actual scene, however, was shot in a stationary van. Movie grips rocked the vehicle to make it seem like the car was actually in motion.

I suspect that creating this scene made the Beatles so hungry that they needed some of these delightful chicken nuggets after shooting. (Coulda happened, right?)

"Let's hope my I Should Have Flown Better turns out better than that."
(Photo courtesy of Photofest)

INGREDIENTS

6 large boneless chicken
   breasts
1 cup (275 ml) Italian-
   seasoned bread crumbs
¹/₂ cup (140 ml) grated
   Parmesan cheese
2 teaspoons salt

2 teaspoons garlic powder
1 cup (235 ml) melted
   salted butter

EQUIPMENT
Large mixing bowl
Large baking sheet
Aluminum foil

Preheat the oven to 400° F (205° C). Cut each chicken breast into 6 nuggets. In a mixing bowl, combine the bread crumbs, grated Parmesan, salt, and garlic powder. Line a baking sheet with aluminum foil. Dip each chicken nugget into the melted butter, then roll it in the bread crumb and cheese mixture. Arrange in a single layer on the baking sheet and bake for 20 to 25 minutes. Serve with a dipping sauce of your choice. Serves 6.

Did you know . . . ?

🍎 On August 14, 1966, the radio station KLUE in Longview, Texas, sponsored a public bonfire for the burning of Beatles records because of John's misinterpreted "The Beatles are more popular than Jesus" comment. Shortly after the bonfire, the station's broadcast tower was struck by lightning, taking the station off the air. The lightning ruined some of the station's electronic equipment and knocked the news director unconscious. Beatles fans around the world felt vindicated.

Kansas City Chicken and Rice

("Kansas City")

I'm goin' to Kansas City, Kansas City here I come . . . for some of this fabulous chicken and peppers. Wanna come? (Contributed by Lee Mandato.)

INGREDIENTS
- 2 tablespoons olive oil
- 3 large green peppers, seeded and cut into strips
- 1/2 cup (140 ml) chopped onion
- 2 pounds (900 g) boneless chicken breast, boiled, skinned, and cut into 1/2 × 2 inch (13 × 50 mm) strips

- 1 cup (235 ml) chicken stock
- 2 tablespoons cornstarch
  Soy sauce to taste

EQUIPMENT
Electric skillet
Mixing bowl

Heat the olive oil in an electric skillet. Sauté the green peppers and onion in the oil until the peppers are tender. Add the chicken to the skillet. In a mixing bowl, stir together the chicken stock and cornstarch until somewhat thick. Add this mixture to the skillet and stir. Add a splash of soy sauce to the skillet to taste. Simmer, covered, for 15 minutes. Serve hot over plain white rice. Serves 4 to 6.

"Kansas City Chicken and Rice, here I come!" (Photo courtesy of Photofest)

We Can Wok It Out

("We Can Work It Out")

"Life . . . is . . . ve-ry . . . short . . . and there's no tiiiiime . . ." so try this quick and delicious chicken stir-fry. Your dinner guests will undoubtedly "think that it's all right"!

INGREDIENTS

 3 tablespoons peanut oil
12 ounces (340 g) boneless, skinless chicken breasts, cut into strips
 1 green pepper, seeded and cut into strips
½ cup (115 g) carrots, sliced very thin
¾ cup (170 g) cabbage, shredded fine

 1 8-ounce (225 g) can pineapple chunks in natural juices
¼ cup (60 g) water chestnuts, sliced
 2 teaspoons soy sauce
 1 tablespoon white wine vinegar

EQUIPMENT
Large wok or skillet

Heat 2 tablespoons of the peanut oil in a large wok or skillet. Add the chicken and fry the pieces until they are completely white. (No pink should be seen.) Remove the chicken strips from the wok and set aside. Add the remaining peanut oil to the wok, then quickly add the pepper and carrots and stir-fry for 2 minutes. Add the shredded cabbage to the wok and stir-fry for 1 minute more. Add the chicken strips to the wok and stir in the pineapple chunks (with the juice), water chestnuts, soy sauce, and white wine vinegar. Simmer slowly for 3 more minutes and serve hot over boiled white rice. Serves 4.

Any Thyme at All

("Any Time at All")

"Any Time at All" was, according to John, an attempt at "rewriting" the song "It Won't Be Long." (Both have the same tried-and-true rock-chord pattern of C to A minor.)

In the song's honor, feel free to enjoy this wonderful chicken and rice dish "any time at all."

INGREDIENTS

- 2 tablespoons (¼ stick) salted butter
- 2 tablespoons (30 g) all-purpose flour
- 1 cup (235 ml) chicken stock
- 1 cup (235 ml) milk
- 12–14 ounces (340–400 g) chicken meat, boiled and, cut into 2-inch (5 cm) strips
- 1 4-ounce (115 g) can kitchen-cut green beans, drained
- 2 tablespoons lemon juice
- Pinch dried thyme
- Salt and black pepper to taste
- ³/₄ cup (170 g) Minute Rice
- 1 tablespoon parsley
- ½ cup (115 g) carrots, peeled, blanched, and cut into 1-inch (25 mm) strips
- Grated carrot for garnish

EQUIPMENT

Large skillet

In a large skillet, melt the butter. Stir in the flour and whisk together for approximately 1 minute. Whisk in the chicken stock and milk and bring to a boil. Simmer gently, stirring continuously, until the sauce begins to thicken. Stir in the chicken strips, green beans, lemon juice, thyme, and salt and pepper to taste. Cook for 10 minutes over medium heat, until the chicken is heated through.

While the chicken is cooking, prepare the rice. Toss the cooked rice with parsley and arrange it in the center of a serving dish. Add the carrot strips to the skillet a couple of minutes before the chicken is finished and toss well. Pour the cooked chicken mixture on top of the rice and garnish with grated carrot. Serves 4.

Turkey to Ride

("Ticket to Ride")

I think I'm gonna be sad . . . if you don't try this delicious turkey recipe for your next Beatles Thanksgiving or holiday feast!

INGREDIENTS

STUFFING

- ³/₄ *pound (3 sticks) salted butter*
- 18 *medium onions, peeled, boiled until barely tender, drained, and chopped*
- ³/₄ *cup (210 ml) fine-chopped celery*
- 6 *cups (1,650 ml) dry Italian-flavored bread crumbs*
- 6 *cups (1,650 ml) corn-bread crumbs*
- ³/₄ *teaspoon black pepper*
- ³/₄ *cup (180 ml) chicken broth Salt to taste*

TURKEY

- *12-pound (5.4 kg) turkey*
- ¹/₂ *pound (2 sticks) salted butter Salt Black pepper*
- ¹/₄ *cup (60 ml) water for basting*

EQUIPMENT

Large skillet
Large mixing bowl
Pastry brush
V-shaped roasting rack in a roasting pan
Aluminum foil
Meat thermometer

Make the stuffing: In a large skillet, melt the butter. Stir in the onions, celery, and chicken broth, and cook over low heat until the onions are soft. Pour both kinds of bread crumbs into a large mixing bowl. Add the onion-and-celery mixture and toss lightly until the blend reaches stuffing consistency. Add salt and pepper to taste. Makes 9 cups (2.1 l)—enough for a 12-pound (5.4 kg) turkey.

Stuff and roast the turkey: Preheat the oven to 325° F (163° C). Rinse the turkey with cold water and pat it dry. Stuff the body and neck cavity of the bird with the previously prepared onion stuffing. Melt about half of the butter in a skillet and use a pastry brush to baste the outside of the turkey with the melted butter. Sprinkle salt and pepper on the turkey. Cover the V-shaped rack with greased aluminum foil. Place the turkey, breast down, on the rack in a roasting pan. Place the turkey in the preheated oven. Melt the remaining butter in a skillet with $1/4$ cup (60 ml) of water; use this to baste the turkey every 20 minutes while it bakes until enough pan drippings to baste with have accumulated in the bottom of the roasting pan. Cook the turkey for a little over 1 hour and then turn it over, so that it is breast up. Cook for 2 more hours, until a meat thermometer reads 170° F (77° C) in the breast meat and 185° F (85° C) in the thigh meat. (You should cook turkey for 15 minutes per pound if it weighs less than 16 pounds/7.2 kg; 12 minutes per pound if it weighs more.) Remove the turkey from the oven and cover it with aluminum foil on a warm platter. Let stand for 15 minutes before carving. Serve with turkey gravy, a garden salad, roasted potatoes, green beans, and dinner rolls. Serves 10 to 12.

A John Lennon Grocery List

In 1979 Frederic Seaman was hired as John Lennon's personal assistant; he was working for John at the time of John's death in December 1980.

Seaman was John's private secretary, driver, personal assistant, companion, and often served as John's only connection with the world outside the ex-Beatle's Dakota Arms apartment.

In his fascinating 1991 book, *The Last Days of John Lennon,* Seaman recounts the day-to-day activities of John in his final months on earth.

John would usually leave Seaman a lengthy memo each morning with instructions for things John wanted done. Buying books, organizing files, helping Sean with something, dealing with repair people, and other mundane duties were often assigned to Seaman, who tried to follow John's instructions to the letter. Once, when Seaman did *not* follow John's instructions to the letter, John left him a scathing note commanding him not to "improvise"—to just "PLAY THE NOTES!"

One of Seaman's duties included personally grocery shopping for John. John would make up his own shopping list (which was apparently separate from the household's shopping needs), and Seaman would go out and specifically buy what John wanted.

Since this is a book of Beatle recipes, I thought that one of John Lennon's typical grocery lists would be of interest to all you Fab Four Foodies out there. (NOTE: John's love for his cats was intense: You'll notice he placed *their* food needs at the top of his list!)

CAT LITTER (URGENT)
CALVES LIVER + FRESH HAMBURGER MEAT
RICE
HONEY BRAN MUFFINS
MUSHROOMS
CABBAGE
FISH
SOME GLUES FOR DAD + SEAN
BANANAS. ONE BUNCH

The Long and Winding Ragout

("The Long and Winding Road")

Paul was outraged at the syrupy strings accompaniment Phil Spector overdubbed onto Paul's piano and vocal track for this song, but his fury was ignored: The "Spectorized" version is the one that ended up on the *Let It Be* album.

This recipe is dedicated to Paul's original version of "The Long and Winding Road." (Check out *Anthology 3* for a poignant performance of the song presented—as the liner notes indicate—"as nature intended.")

INGREDIENTS
- ¹/₄ cup (¹/₂ stick) salted butter
- 2 onions, chopped
- 1 tablespoon (15 g) all-purpose flour
- 2 teaspoons chili powder
- 1 14-ounce (415 ml) can tomatoes, crushed
- 1 tablespoon Worcestershire sauce
- 2 tablespoons tomato puree (or 1 tablespoon tomato paste)
- 1 cup (235 ml) turkey stock
- 2 teaspoons sugar
- 1 bay leaf
- Salt and black pepper to taste
- 1 pound (450 g) cooked turkey breast, diced
- 1 7-ounce (200 g) can pimientos, drained and chopped
- 1 7-ounce (200 g) can red kidney beans, drained

EQUIPMENT
Large saucepan
Large skillet

Melt half the butter in a large saucepan. Fry the onions in the butter until they are soft, but do not let them brown. Stir in the flour and chili powder and cook for 1 minute. Add to the pan the crushed tomatoes, Worcestershire sauce, tomato puree, turkey stock, sugar, and bay leaf, and stir. Season to taste with salt and black pepper. Bring the contents of the pot to a boil and simmer, covered, for 30 minutes. While the tomato sauce is simmering, fry the cooked turkey breast in the remaining butter. Add the turkey, pimientos, and kidney beans to the tomato sauce and simmer for 10 more minutes. Serve with French bread. Serves 4.

Did you know . . . ?

 John played the bass part on Paul's song "The Long and Winding Road."

(Photo courtesy of Photofest)

Fab Four
Fish Fare

Crabalocker Fettuccine

("I Am the Walrus")

John's brilliant "I Am the Walrus" was a real mélange of musical ingredients, including lyrics inspired by two acid trips and a poem from *Alice in Wonderland.*

This delicious seafood and pasta dish is likewise a mélange of ingredients—and just as John's ingredients blended beautifully in the final song, so these ingredients combine to make a delicious and hearty main dish for fish (and walrus) lovers!

INGREDIENTS

- 1 tablespoon olive oil
- 8 scallions, sliced thin
- 3 garlic cloves, minced
- $^1/_2$ pound (225 g) cooked peeled shrimp
- $^1/_2$ pound (225 g) cooked crabmeat, flaked
- 2 tablespoons dry white wine
- 1 tablespoon lemon juice
- $^1/_4$ teaspoon crushed red pepper flakes
- $^1/_4$ teaspoon dried thyme
- $^1/_4$ teaspoon salt
- 2 cups (550 ml) cooked fettuccine (approximately 4 ounces/115 g uncooked noodles)

EQUIPMENT

Large skillet
Large serving bowl

In a large skillet, heat the olive oil. Add the scallions and garlic and cook until the scallions are soft. Add the shrimp, crabmeat, white wine, lemon juice, red pepper, dried thyme, and salt. Cook for approximately 3 to 4 minutes, stirring constantly. Pour the contents of the skillet over the cooked fettuccine and mix. Serve with a tossed salad and hot garlic bread. Serves 4.

Bay (Scallops) Tripper (Yeah!)

("Day Tripper")

This tangy broiled bay scallops recipe will delight you so much you definitely will not want to make it a "one night stand."

INGREDIENTS

Nonstick vegetable cooking spray or vegetable shortening

1 pound (450 g) fresh bay scallops

1 8-ounce (235 ml) bottle French dressing

Italian-seasoned bread crumbs for coating

EQUIPMENT

2 large bowls for dipping and coating

9 × 9 inch (23 × 23 cm) baking dish

Preheat the broiler. Either grease the baking dish or spray it with a nonstick vegetable cooking spray. Dip each bay scallop in the French dressing and then roll it around in the seasoned bread crumbs until it is completely coated. Arrange the scallops in the baking dish and broil for approximately 7 minutes, until the coating is browned. (Bay scallops cook quickly. Do not overcook.) Serve immediately with coleslaw and baked potatoes. Serves 2 to 4.

Did you know . . . ?

 "Day Tripper" may claim the most eclectic set of admirers of all of the Fabs' songs. Cover versions of the kick-ass rocker have been recorded by such disparate artists as Otis Redding, Nancy Sinatra, James Taylor, Anne Murray, Whitesnake, Cheap Trick, Jimi Hendrix, 10CC, Lulu, and, horrors of horrors, Mae West.

Rubber Sole Fillets

(Rubber Soul)

Don't worry: This delicious sole recipe is anything but rubbery—and it makes a perfect accompaniment to an all-night *Rubber Soul* listening party.

INGREDIENTS
- 4 *sole fillets*
- *Salt and black pepper*
- *Dash ground nutmeg*
- 2 *tablespoons parsley*
- $^1/_4$ *cup ($^1/_2$ stick) salted butter*
- $^1/_2$ *cup (120 ml) dry white wine*
- 1 *tablespoon olive oil*
- 4 *onions, sliced*
- 1 *teaspoon lemon juice*

EQUIPMENT
- *9 × 12 inch (23 × 30 cm) baking dish*
- *Aluminum foil*
- *Medium skillet*
- *Slotted spoon*
- *Paper towels*

Preheat the oven to 350° F (177° C). Season the sole fillets with salt, pepper, nutmeg, and half of the parsley. Put 2 small dabs of butter on top of each fillet. Pour the white wine over the fillets, cover, and bake for 30 minutes. While the fillets are baking, heat the remaining butter and the olive oil in a skillet. Add the onions to the skillet and sauté until they are soft and golden brown. Scoop the onions out of the oil with a slotted spoon and drain well on a paper-towel-lined dish. Spread the onions around the fillets about 1 minute before the fish will be done. When the fillets are finished cooking, sprinkle on the remaining parsley and the lemon juice and serve immediately. Serves 4.

I'd Love to Tuna You On

("A Day in the Life")

"A Day in the Life" was a brilliant collaborative effort between John Lennon and Paul McCartney. According to legend, John came to Paul with the "I read the news today oh boy" verses, and Paul was instantly captivated. According to Mr. McCartney, he couldn't wait to get his hands on the tune and see what else could be done with it. Fortuitously, Paul had been working on a song that began, "Woke up, fell out of bed," and after playing around with the two parts, John and Paul realized that Paul's unfinished song would fit seamlessly into John's song. And thus, a *Sgt. Pepper* masterpiece was born.

This "I Love to Tuna You On" casserole is a tribute to one *fine* piece of songwriting.

INGREDIENTS
- $^{1}/_{2}$ pound (225 g) elbow pasta, cooked to al dente consistency and drained
- 2 $6^{1}/_{2}$-ounce (185 g) cans solid white tuna, drained and lightly flaked
- 12 ounces (360 ml) sour cream
- $^{3}/_{4}$ cup (180 ml) milk
- 1 3-ounce (90 g) can sliced mushrooms, drained
  Salt to taste
- $^{1}/_{4}$ teaspoon black pepper
- $^{1}/_{4}$ cup (70 ml) Italian-seasoned bread crumbs
- $^{1}/_{4}$ cup (70 ml) grated Parmesan cheese
- 2 tablespoons ($^{1}/_{4}$ stick) salted butter, melted
  Paprika

EQUIPMENT
Large pot
2-quart (1.9 l) casserole baking dish
Mixing bowl

After draining the elbow pasta, return it to the pot. Preheat the oven to 350° F (177° C). Add to the pasta the tuna, sour cream, milk, mushrooms, salt, and pepper. Mix well. Pour the contents of the pot into an ungreased casserole baking dish. In a separate bowl, mix the bread crumbs, Parmesan cheese, and melted butter. Sprinkle this mixture over the casserole. Sprinkle paprika on top of the bread crumb mixture and bake for 35 to 40 minutes, until the cheese bubbles. Serve with a tossed salad and French bread. Serves 6 to 8.

Did you know . . . ?

🍎 John got the "four thousand holes in Blackburn, Lancashire," line in "A Day in the Life" from a news story in the January 17, 1967, issue of the London *Daily Mail.* The paper was propped up on his piano as he was fooling around and the line just leaped out at him. The *Daily Mail* story began, "There are 4,000 holes in the road in Blackburn, Lancashire, or one twenty-sixth of a hole per person, according to a council survey. If Blackburn is typical there are two million holes in Britain's roads and 300,000 in London."

The Scallops of John and Yoko

("The Ballad of John and Yoko")

The John Lennon song "The Ballad of John and Yoko" (which was, of course, about his and Yoko's wedding and the days that followed) was released as a Beatles single and is one of the more unusual Beatles recordings. Why? Because it featured only John and Paul, who played all the instruments and did all the singing (George and Ringo were nowhere to be found), and it was the first Beatles single to actually be released in stereo. (The B side of this single was George Harrison's "Old Brown Shoe," though, which featured all four Fabs as well as Billy Preston on the organ.)

From what I've heard, this delicious baked scallops recipe is available "in Gibraltar near Spain," and maybe even in "the Amsterdam Hilton"!

INGREDIENTS

1 tablespoon salted butter
1 green pepper, seeded and cut into chunks
1 onion, chopped
6 celery stalks, chopped
2 pounds (900 g) scallops, cut into ³/₄-inch (19 mm) pieces
1 10¹/₂-ounce (310 ml) can condensed cream of mushroom soup
¹/₄ teaspoon ground nutmeg
¹/₄ teaspoon paprika
1 tablespoon lemon juice
Salt and black pepper to taste
1 3-ounce (90 g) can sliced mushrooms, drained
1 cup (275 ml) Italian-seasoned bread crumbs
1 cup (275 ml) shredded Swiss cheese
Parsley for garnish

EQUIPMENT
Large skillet
Large casserole baking dish

Preheat the oven to 350° F (177° C). Heat the butter in a large skillet, and sauté the green pepper, onion, and celery until they are all tender. Add the scallops and stir. Add the mushroom soup, nutmeg, paprika, lemon juice, and salt and pepper to taste. Cook, uncovered, for 10 minutes. Add the sliced mushrooms. Pour the contents of the skillet into a buttered casserole baking dish. Top with the bread crumbs and shredded Swiss cheese and bake, uncovered, for 25 minutes. Garnish with parsley and serve with baked potatoes. Serves 6.

Did you know . . . ?

🍎 In the spring of 1970, John Lennon was asked to play the role of Jesus Christ in a pop musical called *Jesus Christ* scheduled to debut at St. Paul's Cathedral in London. John agreed to play the part—on the condition that Yoko Ono be hired to play the part of Mary Magdalene. Neither John nor Yoko ended up appearing in the musical.

We Shall Shrimp and Save

("When I'm Sixty-Four")

If you get a "yes" answer when you sing to your loved one, "Will you still feed me?" make a point of then requesting this delicious shrimp scampi primavera dish . . . complete with the "bottle of wine" so you won't be "wasting away!"

INGREDIENTS

- ³/₄ cup (180 ml) olive oil
- 2 tablespoons minced garlic
- ¹/₂ teaspoon fresh lemon peel, chopped fine
- 2 carrots, cut into 2 × ¹/₄ inch (50 × 6 mm) strips
- 1 8-ounce (225 g) zucchini, cut into 2 × ¹/₄ inch (50 × 6 mm) strips
- 1 medium red pepper, seeded and cut into 2 × ¹/₄ inch (50 × 6 mm) strips
- 1¹/₂ pounds (675 g) medium shrimp, cleaned

- 2 tablespoons lemon juice
- ³/₄ teaspoon salt
- ¹/₈ teaspoon black pepper
- 2 tablespoons torn fresh Italian parsley
- 2 teaspoons dried basil
- 1 pound (450 g) linguine or spaghetti, cooked and kept hot

EQUIPMENT
Large skillet

In a large skillet, heat the olive oil. Add the minced garlic and chopped lemon peel and cook together, stirring continuously, for 30 seconds. Add the carrots, zucchini, red pepper, and shrimp to the skillet and cook over medium heat, stirring often, for 3 to 4 minutes, until the shrimp turns pink. Sprinkle the cooked shrimp with the lemon juice, salt, and pepper, and then stir in the parsley and basil. Pour the scampi over the drained linguine or spaghetti and toss well. Serve immediately. Serves 8.

The boys appear to be looking around 'round 'round for some flounder.
(Photo courtesy of Photofest)

Look Around 'Round 'Round Flounder

("Dear Prudence")

Make sure you carefully look around 'round 'round the fish case when you pick out the flounder fillets for this tasty dish! Always buy the freshest fish you can find: It'd make Prudence very happy.

INGREDIENTS
  5 tablespoons salted butter
 $1/3$ cup (90 ml) chopped onion
  1 cup (275 ml) wheat crumbs
    (substitute seasoned bread
    crumbs if wheat crumbs are
    not available)
 $1/2$ teaspoon grated lemon peel
  1 tablespoon parsley
 $1/4$ teaspoon celery seeds
    Dash black pepper

  2 tablespoons lemon juice
  6 large flounder fillets
    Butter-flavored nonstick
    vegetable cooking spray
    Parsley sprigs and lemon
    slices for garnish

EQUIPMENT
Large skillet
Toothpicks
Large casserole baking dish

Preheat the oven to 350° F (177° C). Melt 4 tablespoons of the butter in a large skillet. Sauté the chopped onion in the butter until tender, approximately 5 minutes. Remove the cooked onion from the heat and add the wheat crumbs, lemon peel, parsley, celery seeds, black pepper, and lemon juice. Stir well to combine.

Lay the flounder fillets out flat and spoon 3 to 4 tablespoons of the stuffing onto the large end of each fillet. Roll up the fillets tightly and secure each with toothpicks.

Spray a large casserole baking dish with butter-flavored vegetable cooking spray and place the fillets in the dish. Melt the remaining tablespoon of butter and drizzle it over the fillets. Bake for 30 minutes, until the fish flakes easily. Garnish the baked fillets with parsley sprigs and lemon slices and serve with a garden salad and potato dish of your choice. Serves 6.

Stuff, Stuff Me Do!

("Love Me Do")

"Love Me Do" was the Beatles' first single, and they were all in their early twenties when they recorded it. George Martin didn't like Ringo's drumming on the track, so he made them record a second version with Andy White playing the drums. Ringo played the tambourine on this second version; ultimately, both versions were released. George Martin decided to substitute the Andy White version on the LP—*after* the Ringo version had been released as a single. You can tell the difference by the presence—or lack of—Ringo's tambourine.

This fabulous stuffed shrimp dish is included to honor this first Beatles single. (The connection? I'm making a snide comment about Andy White being "stuffed" down the Beatles' throats due to one of George Martin's rare misjudgments about the group's sound.)

INGREDIENTS
1 pound (450 g) jumbo shrimp, cleaned and deveined
1 cup (2 sticks) salted butter
1 15-ounce (430 g) can Italian-flavored bread crumbs
Juice of 1 medium lemon

EQUIPMENT
Large skillet
9 × 9 inch (23 × 23 cm) baking dish

Split each shrimp almost entirely in half lengthwise and set aside. Preheat the oven to 450° F (232° C). In a large skillet, melt the butter. Add the bread crumbs and toss lightly until the mixture begins to thicken into a stuffing. Squeeze the lemon over the mixture and add enough water to make the stuffing a little sticky so it will be easy to pack. Place 1 heaping tablespoon of stuffing on top of each shrimp and arrange the stuffed shrimp in a baking dish. Bake for 15 minutes. Serve with lemon wedges and melted butter for dipping. Serves 2 to 4.

Jojo's Jambalaya

("Get Back")

This dish is why Jojo left his home in Tucson, Arizona, and moved to California: That's where he first tasted this incredible shrimp entrée!

INGREDIENTS

- 3 slices bacon, fried and diced
- $1/2$ cup (140 ml) chopped onion
- $1/2$ cup (140 ml) chopped green pepper
- $1/2$ cup (140 ml) chopped celery
- 1 tablespoon minced garlic
- 4 cups (950 ml) canned tomatoes, with liquid
- $1/8$ teaspoon cayenne pepper
- 1 teaspoon chili powder
- $1/4$ teaspoon dried thyme
- 2 pounds (900 g) shrimp, cooked, shelled, and deveined
- $1/4$ cup (70 ml) fine-chopped fresh parsley
  Salt to taste
- 4 cups (1,100 ml) cooked Minute Rice, kept hot

EQUIPMENT

Large skillet
Paper towels
Large serving platter

In a large skillet, fry the bacon until crisp. Remove the bacon from the skillet and drain on paper towels. In the same skillet, cook the onion, green pepper, and celery in the bacon fat over medium heat until the onion is soft. Add to the skillet the garlic, canned tomatoes with their liquid, cayenne pepper, chili powder, and thyme, and simmer over low heat for 20 minutes. Add the cooked shrimp, parsley, and salt to the skillet and cook until the shrimp is hot. Mound the hot Minute Rice on a large serving platter and spoon the shrimp and tomato sauce on top of it. Garnish the shrimp with the crisp bacon. Serve with a garden salad. Serves 6.

For You Bluefish

("For You Blue")

"For You Blue" was written by George for his wife at the time, Pattie Boyd Harrison. Some Beatles insiders have speculated that if Pattie and George had shared this fabulous bluefish dish, the marriage might have survived. Never underestimate the power of bluefish.

INGREDIENTS
- 6 medium Idaho or russet potatoes
- 2½ (1.1 kg) pounds large bluefish fillets
- 1 green pepper, sliced
- 2 tomatoes, sliced
- ¼ pound (115 g) sliced bacon, cut into 1-inch (25 mm) long pieces
- 1 teaspoon paprika
- 1 cup (235 ml) sour cream, at room temperature

EQUIPMENT
Large saucepan
Large casserole baking dish

Preheat the oven to 400° F (205° C). Peel and cut the potatoes into 1/4-inch (6 mm) slices. Boil the potato slices in salted water for 5 minutes. Drain the slices and spread them over the bottom of a large buttered baking dish. Cut slashes in the bluefish fillets about 1/2 to 3/4 inch (13 to 19 mm) apart. In each slash insert a slice of pepper, a slice of tomato, and a slice of bacon. Spread the fish fillets on top of the potatoes and sprinkle with the paprika. Bake for 20 minutes. Spread the sour cream on top of the fillets and bake for 5 minutes more. Serves 6.

Did you know . . . ?

🍎 George Harrison is a competent violinist; he played violin on "All You Need Is Love" and "Don't Pass Me By."

"Toppermost of the Poppermost" Pasta Dishes

Give (Pasta and) Peas a Chance

("Give Peace a Chance")

"All we are sa-a-a-ying . . ." is give this classic, hearty Italian dish a chance!

INGREDIENTS

1 large onion
2 tablespoons olive oil
3 slices Canadian bacon, cut up into bite-sized pieces
1 14.9-ounce (430 g) can of peas (retain water)
1 8-ounce (225 g) can of peas (drain water)
   Garlic powder, salt, pepper, and grated cheese to taste

2 medium eggs, beaten
$^1/_2$ pound (225 g) spaghetti (broken in half)

EQUIPMENT

Large skillet with cover
Small bowl
Large deep pot for boiling pasta

Sauté the onion in the olive oil in a covered skillet until it's soft. Add the Canadian bacon to the pan and cook, uncovered, until the bacon is tender. Slowly add the 2 cans of peas, including the water from the larger can, to the onions and bacon. In a small bowl, add salt, pepper, and grated cheese to taste to the 2 beaten eggs. When the pea-and-onion mixture begins to boil, add the seasoned eggs to the skillet. Add a dash of garlic powder to taste and cook this mixture for about 10 minutes. While this is cooking, boil the spaghetti to al dente texture in a large deep pot. Drain the spaghetti and add the pea-and-onion mixture to it. Toss together and serve with more grated cheese and a green salad. Serves 4.

I'm a Lasagna

("I'm a Loser")

This classic, hearty Italian dish is the ultimate Sunday dinner. Put on the *White Album* and let your repast last from "Back in the U.S.S.R." to "Good Night"! This dish can be made with either a plain tomato sauce or a meat sauce (both recipes are provided here), and the lasagna itself can also be made meatless if desired. (The recipe assumes it will be made with meat. If you're a veggie, just leave the meat out and use the plain tomato sauce.)

CLASSIC ITALIAN TOMATO SAUCE

INGREDIENTS
2 tablespoons olive oil
$^3/_4$ cup (180 ml) tomato paste
$2^1/_2$ cups (590 ml) canned
    tomatoes, crushed
1 teaspoon sugar

$^1/_2$ teaspoon black pepper
1 tablespoon dried basil
    Salt to taste

EQUIPMENT
Large saucepan

Heat the olive oil in a saucepan. Slowly stir in the tomato paste, crushed tomatoes, sugar, pepper, and basil. Simmer for 30 minutes, stirring occasionally. Add a little wine or water if the sauce becomes too thick. Cook for another 15 minutes and then stir in the salt.

CLASSIC ITALIAN MEAT SAUCE

Start with the recipe for Classic Italian Tomato Sauce, except cook 1 pound (450 g) of ground beef in the heated oil before adding the tomatoes and other ingredients. You can also add pieces of ground sausage or veal, or chopped onion, for extra flavor.

I'M A LASAGNA

INGREDIENTS
1   1-pound (450 g) package
    lasagna noodles
2   medium eggs, beaten
1   pound (450 g) ricotta cheese
2   tablespoons oregano (Italian
    seasoning blend can be
    substituted)
1   teaspoon salt
$1/2$ teaspoon garlic powder
$1/8$ teaspoon pepper
5   cups (1,175 ml) Classic
    Italian Tomato Sauce or
    Classic Italian Meat Sauce

1   pound (450 g) mozzarella
    cheese, sliced thin
$1/2$ pound (225 g) ground beef,
    cooked (optional)
$1/2$ pound (225 g) Italian sausage,
    cooked (optional)
1   cup (275 ml) grated Parmesan
    cheese

EQUIPMENT
Large saucepan
Large mixing bowl
Large baking dish
Aluminum foil

Cook the lasagna noodles according to the directions on the package, drain, and set aside. Preheat the oven to 400° F (205° C). In a large mixing bowl, mix the eggs, ricotta, oregano (or Italian seasoning), salt, garlic powder, and pepper. Spread 1/2 cup (120 ml) of the tomato sauce of your choice on the bottom of a large baking dish. Neatly arrange one-third of the lasagna noodles on top of the tomato sauce, covering the sauce completely. Spoon onto the noodles half of the mozzarella slices, half of the ricotta cheese mixture, and half of the cooked beef and sausage. Pour $1^1/2$ cups (355 ml) of tomato sauce on top of this layer. Sprinkle one-third of the Parmesan cheese on top of the sauce. Repeat the layers. Top with the remaining lasagna noodles, tomato sauce, and grated cheese. Cover tightly with aluminum foil and bake for 40 minutes. Remove the foil and bake for another 20 minutes. Let the lasagna sit for 5 minutes or so to set before serving. Serve with a tossed green salad and garlic bread. Serves 8.

Penne in the Squash With Onions

("Lucy in the Sky With Diamonds")

Me mum invented this dish and every time she serves it, I sing, "Penne in the squash with onions" over and over to her. (Heck, John sings the "Lucy in the Sky With Diamonds" chorus *fifteen times* on the *Sgt. Pepper* album. Aren't I entitled, too?) Me mum is usually less than thrilled—but you will be *delighted* once you get a taste of this incredible pasta dish!

INGREDIENTS
- 6 *large green squash*
  Olive-oil-flavored nonstick vegetable spray
- 6 *tablespoons olive oil*
  Salt to taste
  Dash black pepper
- 1 *large onion, chopped fine*
- 6 *garlic cloves, cut into small pieces*
- 1 *pound (450 g) penne pasta*
- 2 *tablespoons dry white wine*
  Garlic powder to taste

EQUIPMENT
Colander
9 × 12 inch (23 × 30 cm) Pyrex baking dish
Large pot

Preheat the oven to 350° F (177° C). Cut each squash lengthwise into 4 sections. Slice off about half of the pulp from each piece, leaving some pulp on the skin. Cut each squash spear into small pieces, approximately 1/8 inch (3 mm) thick. Place the pieces in a colander and rinse in cold water. Drain well. Spray the baking dish with olive-oil-flavored vegetable spray. Place the squash in the baking dish and drizzle all of the olive oil over it. Add salt and pepper to taste. Bake for approximately 30 minutes, stirring every 10 minutes or so, until the squash is partially cooked. Add the onion, garlic cloves, wine, and garlic powder, mixing well into the squash. Cook, uncovered, for another 25 to 30 minutes. When the squash and onion are almost cooked, boil the pasta to an al dente consistency, drain, and return it to the pot. Pour the cooked squash and onion over the penne and mix well. Serve immediately with a tossed salad, grated Parmesan cheese, and garlic bread. Serves 4 to 6.

Get Baked!

("Get Back")

This irresistible, classic baked ziti recipe will convince you that even though Jojo lived in Tucson, Arizona, there's no doubt he was actually a full-blooded Italian—with impeccable taste in cuisine to boot!

INGREDIENTS

- 2 cups (475 ml) Classic Italian Tomato Sauce or Meat Sauce (see page 144)
- 1 pound (450 g) ziti, boiled to al dente consistency and drained
- 1 pound (450 g) ground beef, sautéed with garlic powder, salt, and black pepper
- 1 pound (450 g) ground sausage, sautéed
- 8 ounces (225 g) shredded mozzarella cheese
- 1 pound (450 g) ricotta cheese
  Grated Parmesan cheese
  Salt and black pepper to taste

EQUIPMENT
Large casserole baking dish

Preheat the oven to 350° F (177° C). Spread a thin layer of tomato sauce on the bottom of a large baking dish. Add the entire pound of cooked ziti, the cooked ground beef, the cooked ground sausage, the shredded mozzarella, and the pound of ricotta. Toss together to blend. Top with more tomato sauce, sprinkle generously with grated Parmesan cheese, add salt and pepper to taste, and bake for 30 minutes. Serve with a tossed garden salad and garlic bread. Serves 6 to 8.

Here's the scoop: Eleanor Rigatoni is fab! (Photo courtesy of Photofest)

Eleanor Rigatoni

("Eleanor Rigby")

We suspect that Eleanor Rigby might not have been so lonely if she had cooked up a batch of this delicious seafood pasta dish and invited Father McKenzie and a few of his parishioners over to chow down with her!

INGREDIENTS
- 3 tablespoons olive oil
- 3 garlic cloves, crushed
- 3 cups (710 ml) Italian-style canned tomatoes, coarsely chopped
- $^1/_4$ cup (60 ml) dry red wine
- $^1/_2$ teaspoon oregano
- $^1/_2$ teaspoon salt
- $^1/_8$ teaspoon black pepper
- 8 ounces (225 g) rigatoni pasta
- $1^1/_2$ pounds (675 g) shelled shrimp
- $^3/_4$ pound (340 g) sea scallops
- 4 ounces (115 g) mozzarella cheese, sliced thin

EQUIPMENT
Medium saucepan
Large pot
Large casserole baking dish

In a medium saucepan, heat the olive oil. Sauté the garlic until tender, then add the chopped tomatoes, red wine, oregano, salt, and black pepper. Cook this sauce for 30 minutes, stirring occasionally. Preheat the oven to 400° F (205° C). Boil the rigatoni to al dente consistency. Drain the pasta and place it in a large casserole baking dish. Pour the tomato sauce over the pasta and mix together. Add the shrimp and scallops and mix well. Lay the slices of mozzarella on top of the casserole and bake, uncovered, for 25 minutes. Serve with a garden salad. Serves 6 to 8.

Did you know . . . ?

- 🍎 "Eleanor Rigby" was the first use of strings as the sole backing for a vocal in a song by a rock group.

Lady Macaroni
("Lady Madonna")

This inexpensive but hearty dish would surely help our friend Lady Madonna "feed the rest"! It's a wonder how she manages to make ends meet.

INGREDIENTS
- ½ pound (225 g) American cheese, cut into chunks
- ¼ pound (115 g) sharp provolone cheese, shredded
- 1 pound (450 g) elbow pasta, cooked

- 1 quart (950 ml) milk
- Grated Parmesan cheese to taste
- Black pepper

EQUIPMENT
Large casserole baking dish

Preheat the oven to 350° F (177° C). Fill the bottom half of a buttered casserole baking dish with all of the American cheese and half of the provolone cheese. Add the cooked elbow pasta and mix well. Add the milk, the remaining cheese, and the grated Parmesan; mix well. Sprinkle black pepper on top of the casserole and bake uncovered for 1½ hours. Serve with a tossed green salad and French bread. Serves 6 to 8.

Did you know . . . ?

- When Mae West was first approached for permission for her photo to appear on the front cover of the *Sgt. Pepper* album, she refused, reportedly saying, "What would I be doing in a lonely hearts club band?" She ultimately relented, however, after each of the four Beatles wrote her a personal letter requesting her participation. Those letters—which would be incredibly valuable today—have apparently never surfaced (yet) in the collectors' market.

All My Linguine
("All My Loving")

"All My Loving" was one of the first Beatles songs to become a standard; to this day, you can often hear a pasteurized instrumental version of it in the elevator of your choice. In its original version, though, this tune is classic Paul McCartney, and its opening a cappella "Close your (eyes)" foreshadowed the same introductory musical device Paul would use years later in "Hey Jude."

This "All My Linguine" recipe is a classic Italian "white sauce" pasta dish. Considering that "All My Loving" is about kissing, if you're going to take Paul's musical advice, after eating this, I have one word of my own advice: Mouthwash.

INGREDIENTS

2 tablespoons olive oil

3 tablespoons salted butter

6 garlic cloves, minced

6 $6^1/_2$-ounce (185 g each) cans chopped clams

$^1/_2$ cup (140 ml) grated Romano cheese

$1^1/_2$ pounds (675 g) cooked linguine (kept warm)

EQUIPMENT

Large covered skillet

In a large skillet, heat the olive oil and butter. Add the garlic and sauté it until tender. Add the chopped clams with the clam broth and simmer three-quarters covered for approximately 30 minutes. Add the grated Romano and stir until the cheese is melted. Pour the clam sauce over the cooked linguine and serve immediately, with a garden salad and French bread. Serves 6.

Did you know . . . ?

🍎 "All My Loving" was the first song Paul ever wrote by composing the lyrics first and then putting them to music. Prior to this song, he had always written the music and words simultaneously.

This Bowl

("This Boy")

Don't you just love the way John, Paul, and George's harmony vocals blend so beautifully in "This Boy"? Well, you'll also love the way the ingredients of this terrific macaroni and cheese recipe blend to make one memorable dish!

INGREDIENTS

- 2 cups (550 ml) cooked four-color macaroni (approximately 4 ounces/ 115 g uncooked shells)
- 1 tablespoon chopped onion
- 2 tablespoons chopped pimientos
- 2 tablespoons chopped green pepper
- 1 cup (275 ml) diced celery
- 1/3 cup (90 ml) chopped dill pickles
- 1 cup (235 ml) bottled French dressing
- 1/4 cup (60 ml) mayonnaise
- 1 cup (275 ml) shredded extra-sharp cheddar cheese

  Salt and black pepper to taste

  Crisp lettuce leaves to line a large salad bowl

EQUIPMENT

Large mixing bowl
Large salad serving bowl

In a large mixing bowl, combine the cooked pasta, onion, pimientos, green pepper, celery, and pickles. Add the French dressing and toss lightly. Marinate the pasta and vegetables in the French dressing for 10 to 15 minutes, then drain. Add the mayonnaise and shredded cheese. Season to taste with salt and black pepper and toss well. Serve in a large salad bowl lined with lettuce leaves, with garlic bread on the side. Serves 4 to 6.

Lentil Me Your Ears and I'll Sing You a Sausage
("With a Little Help From My Friends")

This simple yet remarkably delicious recipe is Italian through and through—and the perfect musical accompaniment to this delightful entrée would be John's "Sun King" with its made-up Italian lyrics. After all, how can you argue with "Questo obrigado tanta mucho," or "Quando paramucho mi amore," right? Indeed. (Contributed by Mary and Ray Pantalena.)

INGREDIENTS
1 pound (450 g) fresh Italian sausage, cut into bite-sized pieces
6 garlic cloves, minced
1 pound (450 g) small elbow pasta

1 19-ounce (565 ml) can Progresso lentil soup

EQUIPMENT
Large skillet
Large saucepan

Begin frying the sausage pieces in a large skillet. When there is some oil in the skillet, add the minced garlic and continue cooking. Meanwhile, boil the pasta to al dente consistency and keep warm. When the sausage is almost completely cooked, pour off the oil, and add the can of lentil soup to the skillet. Cook the sausage in the lentil soup until the soup is hot. Pour the contents of the skillet over the cooked elbow pasta and mix well. Serve with a green salad, Italian bread, and grated Parmesan. Serves 4 to 6.

(Photo courtesy of Photofest)

"Every Little Thing"
Vegetables and
Side Dishes

You've Got to Fry Your Love Away

("You've Got to Hide Your Love Away")

Here I stand, with skillet in hand . . . and you'll be singing too when you get a taste of real homemade french fries that may steer you away from fast-food fries for good!

INGREDIENTS
- 6 large potatoes
- 2 cups (475 ml) olive oil (approximately)

EQUIPMENT
Large bowl
Paper towels
Large skillet
Frying thermometer
Long fork

Wash and peel the potatoes, then cut them into long strips 1/8 to 1/4 inch (3 to 6 mm) wide. Place the potatoes in a large bowl, cover with cold water, and let them sit for at least 30 minutes. Remove the potatoes from the water and drain on paper towels; pat dry with more paper towels. Heat the olive oil in a skillet until a frying thermometer reads 360° F (183° C). (You will need several inches of oil—add enough to achieve the necessary depth.) Place the potatoes in the oil carefully without crowding. Fry the potatoes until they are a golden brown, moving them around with a long fork until they are evenly cooked. Remove and drain on paper towels. Serve as a side dish with ketchup, mustard, or sour cream. Serves 6.

Did you know . . . ?

🍎 The original title of the Beatles' second movie, *Help!*, was *Eight Arms to Hold You.*

Everybody's Got Something to Hide Except Me and My Dumplings

("Everybody's Got Something to Hide Except Me and My Monkey")

Did you know that one of John's original lines for this song was not "Come on is such a joy," but instead "These dumplings are such a joy"? Really.

INGREDIENTS

2 medium eggs
1 teaspoon salt
$^1/_4$ teaspoon black pepper
$^1/_4$ teaspoon ground nutmeg
$^2/_3$ cup (185 ml) flour
1 tablespoon olive oil
1 cup (275 ml) unsliced bread cut into $^1/_2$-inch (13 mm) cubes

6 medium potatoes, boiled and riced

EQUIPMENT

Small skillet
Large mixing bowl
Potato ricer
Large pot with cover
Slotted spoon

Chill the eggs, salt, pepper, nutmeg, and flour for at least 1 hour. Allow the cooked potatoes to thoroughly cool. Heat the olive oil in a small skillet. Add the bread cubes to the oil and brown on all sides for approximately 3 minutes. Beat the eggs in a large bowl and add the salt, pepper, nutmeg, cooled potatoes, and flour. Blend well. Add more salt and pepper to taste. Form the mixture into balls. Press 2 or 3 browned bread cubes into the center of each potato ball.

Bring a large pot of water to a boil. Drop the potato dumplings into the boiling water, cover, and steam for 15 minutes. Remove the dumplings from the water with a slotted spoon. Serve as a side dish with a dressing of your choice, such as butter, mustard, ketchup, or sour cream. Serves 6.

Did you know . . . ?

🍎 The Beatles song with the longest title is "Everybody's Got Something to Hide Except Me and My Monkey." The songs with the shortest titles are "Girl," "Wait," and "Rain."

Sgt. Pepper's Peppers

("Sgt. Pepper's Lonely Hearts Club Band")

Sgt. Pepper's Lonely Hearts Club Band was the album that changed rock music for all time. It elevated to the level of art a musical form that had previously been dismissed as trite and artless.

And in addition to the enormous impact *Sgt. Pepper* had on the landscape of popular music, the album (and the song) also inspired this fabulous stuffed pepper recipe!

INGREDIENTS
6 large green peppers
1 pound (450 g) ground sirloin
$^1/_2$ cup (140 ml) cooked Minute Rice
$^1/_2$ teaspoon salt
$^1/_4$ teaspoon black pepper
1 medium egg
$^1/_4$ cup (60 ml) milk
$^1/_4$ cup (70 ml) chopped onion

1 cup (235 ml) water
1 $10^1/_2$-ounce (310 ml) can condensed tomato soup

EQUIPMENT
Large mixing bowl
Toothpicks
Large pot

Wash the peppers, cut off their tops, and set the tops aside. Remove the seeds from the peppers and discard. In a large mixing bowl, combine the ground beef, cooked rice, salt, pepper, egg, milk, and chopped onion. Mix thoroughly. Stuff each pepper with this ground beef mixture. Do not overstuff. Replace the tops of the peppers, holding them in place with toothpicks. In a large pot, combine the water and the can of tomato soup. Add the peppers to the pot, cover, and bring the liquid to a boil. Simmer for 1 hour and 15 minutes, basting the peppers several times with the liquid from the pot. Serves 3 to 6.

Did you know . . . ?

- The *Sgt. Pepper's Lonely Hearts Club Band* album took over seven hundred hours to record and cost around $75,000, a steep price considering what the average album of the time cost to produce.

(Photo courtesy of Photofest)

I Am the Eggplant

("I Am the Walrus")

This delicious Italian eggplant dish is best prepared with Beatles music playing in the background. My suggestion is "Magical Mystery Tour": Program the song to repeat on your CD player. The repeated "Roll up" will truly inspire you and add to your cooking experience!

INGREDIENTS
- 2 tablespoons olive oil
- 1 large eggplant
- 2 large eggs, beaten and seasoned with salt and black pepper
- 1/2 cup (140 ml) flour
- 8 ounces (225 g) whole-milk mozzarella, sliced
- 1 pound (450 g) ricotta cheese
- 1 1/2 cups (355 ml) tomato sauce (meatless)
- 1/2 cup (140 ml) grated Parmesan cheese

EQUIPMENT
Skillet
2 large round dishes for dipping (eggs in one, flour in the other)
Paper towels
9 × 12 inch (23 × 30 cm) baking dish

Heat the olive oil in a skillet. Preheat the oven to 350° F (177° C). Peel the eggplant and slice it into 1/8- to 1/4-inch (3 to 6 mm) thick slices. Dip each slice first into the seasoned eggs, then into the flour. Fry each slice in the oil. Drain the cooked slices on sheets of paper towel. Place 1 slice of mozzarella on each slice of eggplant, then spread 1 tablespoon of ricotta on top of the mozzarella. Roll each slice as tightly as possible and place in the baking dish. Pour tomato sauce on top of the rolled slices and sprinkle liberally with grated Parmesan. Bake for 30 minutes. Serve with a side dish of boiled white rice with butter (optional) and crispy Italian or French bread. Serves 4.

Did you know . . . ?

🍎 When John was in his twenties, his favorite food was cornflakes.

Glass Onion Rings

("Glass Onion")

These fab onion rings are best served with bent-backed tulips on the table.

INGREDIENTS
- 4 *large Bermuda onions*
- 2 *cups (475 ml) whole milk*
- *Salt*
- ½ *cup (140 ml) flour*
- 2 *cups (475 ml) olive oil*

EQUIPMENT
- *Shallow dish*
- *Large skillet*
- *Frying thermometer*
- *Long fork*
- *Paper towels*

Peel the skin off the onions and cut them into 1/4-inch (6 mm) slices. Separate the slices by hand into rings. Place the onion rings in a shallow dish and cover with milk. Soak the onion rings in the milk for 30 minutes, turning them over twice as they soak. Add a couple of sprinkles of salt to the flour and dip each onion ring into the flour. Coat each ring thoroughly. Heat the olive oil until it reads 370° F (188° C) on a frying thermometer. Deep-fry several onion rings at a time until they are golden on both sides. Use a long fork to move them around in the oil so that they cook evenly. Remove the rings from the oil and drain them on paper towels. Pat dry with more paper towels if necessary. Sprinkle with salt and serve as a side dish with ketchup or sour cream. Serves 8.

Did you know . . . ?

🍎 John's *Sgt. Pepper* song, "Good Morning, Good Morning," was inspired by a cornflakes commercial playing on television while John was doodling around on the piano one morning.

1, 2, 3, 4-Sided Broccoli Squares

("All Together Now")

In the Beatles' *Yellow Submarine* song "All Together Now"—the inspiration for this delightful recipe—the first line is "1, 2, 3, 4—can I have a little more?" That is exactly what your family will be singing to you once they get a taste of these delicious broccoli and cheese squares!

INGREDIENTS

3 tablespoons olive oil

2 small onions, chopped fine

2 garlic cloves, peeled and minced

1 10-ounce (285 g) package frozen chopped broccoli, thawed

3 medium eggs

³/₄ cup (210 ml) Italian-seasoned bread crumbs

1 8-ounce (225 g) bag shredded sharp cheddar cheese

Grated Parmesan cheese to taste

EQUIPMENT

9 × 12 inch (23 × 30 cm) baking pan

Large skillet

Large mixing bowl

Aluminum foil

Preheat the oven to 350° F (177° C). Grease the baking pan. Heat the olive oil in a large skillet and in it, brown the onions and minced garlic. Add the chopped broccoli and cook until the broccoli is soft. Pour the entire contents of the skillet into a large mixing bowl and add the eggs, bread crumbs, and cheddar cheese; mix well. Pour this mixture into the greased baking pan and sprinkle the grated Parmesan on top. Cover with aluminum foil and bake for 20 minutes. Uncover and bake another 20 minutes, until the top is golden brown. Remove from the oven and let cool. Cut into squares and serve as a vegetable or appetizer. Makes 12 broccoli squares, each 3 × 4 inches (8 × 10 cm).

Carrot That Weight

("Carry That Weight")

This spicy carrot dish will have you singing its praises "a long time"! (Hit it, Ringo!)

INGREDIENTS

- 3 cups (825 ml) cooked carrots, mashed
- 3 medium eggs, beaten
- 2 cups (475 ml) milk
- 4 ounces (115 g) shredded pepperjack cheese
- 1 cup (275 ml) Italian-seasoned bread crumbs
- 2 tablespoons (¹/₄ stick) unsalted butter, melted
- 1 teaspoon prepared horse-radish
- ¹/₄ cup (70 ml) chives, chopped fine
- Salt to taste
- Nonstick cooking spray

EQUIPMENT
9 × 9 inch (23 × 23 cm) baking pan
Large mixing bowl

Preheat the oven to 350° F (177° C). Spray the baking pan with non-stick vegetable cooking spray. In a large bowl, combine the carrots, eggs, milk, cheese, bread crumbs, butter, horseradish, and chives. Mix well. Pour the mixture into the baking pan and bake for 30 minutes. Test the casserole by inserting a knife blade into the center; when the knife comes out clean, it's done. Serve as a vegetarian main dish or cut into squares as a side dish. Serves 8.

Everybody's Trying to Be My Bacon (and String Beans)

("Everybody's Trying to Be My Baby")

Rumor has it that this recipe was inspired by Elvis Presley's version of the song "Everybody's Trying to Be My Baby." Elvis, as you may know, was a rather big bacon fan, but the Beatles stuck to the original version of the song when they performed and recorded it!

INGREDIENTS
- 1 pound (450 g) bacon, cut up into small pieces
- 2 16-ounce (450 g each) cans French-cut green beans (salt-free is okay)
- 1 tablespoon garlic powder

Salt to taste
Black pepper to taste

EQUIPMENT
Large skillet
Large casserole baking dish

In a large skillet, fry the bacon until all the pieces are soft. Add the green beans, garlic powder, and salt and pepper to the skillet. Cover and cook over medium heat for 30 to 40 minutes. Preheat the oven to 350° F (177° C). Transfer the contents of the skillet to a large casserole dish and bake, covered, for 30 minutes, stirring occasionally, until the bacon is crispy. Serve as a side dish. Serves 8.

Bip Bop Broccoli

("Bip Bop")

Okay, so maybe you won't change your mundane day-to-day existence into a *Wild Life* when you make this delightful vegetable dish . . . but you sure will enjoy some good eating! (And yes, I know that "Bip Bop" is an obscure song from one of Wings' lesser-known albums, but my mission here is to inspire, as well as to feed.)

INGREDIENTS
2 *tablespoons olive oil*
2 *tablespoons corn oil*
1 *clove garlic, chopped*
$^1/_4$ *teaspoon crushed red pepper*
1 *bunch fresh broccoli,*
   trimmed and cut into small
   flowerets
   Salt to taste

EQUIPMENT
Large skillet

Heat the olive oil and corn oil in a skillet. Add the garlic and crushed red pepper to the oil and stir. Add the broccoli flowerets to the skillet and mix well so that the flowerets are well coated with oil and seasonings. Sauté over medium heat for 7 to 9 minutes, or until the broccoli is tender. The broccoli should be served crisp—do not overcook. Sprinkle with salt to taste and serve as a side dish. Serves 4.

Arizona Artichoke and Spinach Casserole
("Get Back")

The Beatles were equal-opportunity composers: They paid tribute to their homeland with songs like "Strawberry Fields Forever" and "Penny Lane," but they also broadened their vision to write songs like "Get Back" (which was supposedly written "live" in the studio), in which the main character was born in Tucson, Arizona, in the good ol' U.S. of A.

Bet on it: "Get Back" 's Jojo would love this fabulous baked artichoke and spinach casserole!

INGREDIENTS

Nonstick vegetable cooking spray

1 10-ounce (285 g) can artichoke hearts, drained and cut into quarters

3 10-ounce (285 g each) packages frozen chopped spinach, thawed and drained

1 8-ounce (225 g) package cream cheese

2 tablespoons mayonnaise

6 tablespoons milk

1/2 cup (140 ml) grated Parmesan cheese

EQUIPMENT

Large casserole dish

Mixing bowl

Electric beater

Spray a large casserole dish with vegetable cooking spray. Preheat the oven to 350° F (177° C). Arrange the artichoke hearts on the bottom of the casserole dish. Place the chopped spinach on top of the artichoke hearts. In a mixing bowl, combine the cream cheese, mayonnaise, and milk; beat well with an electric beater. Spread this mixture on top of the spinach, top it liberally with grated Parmesan cheese, and bake for 40 minutes. Serve as a vegetarian main dish or a vegetable side dish. Serves 4 to 6.

Savory Truffles

("Savoy Truffle")

You'll substitute mushrooms for truffles in this delicious recipe . . . unless of course you've got Beatle bucks and can afford (and find!) the real thing.

INGREDIENTS
  3 tablespoons olive oil
  1 onion, chopped
  1 garlic clove, chopped
 12 ounces (340 g) button
    mushrooms, sliced
  1 14-ounce (415 ml) can Italian
    tomatoes, drained and
    chopped

 $^1/_4$ cup (60 ml) dry white wine
 $^1/_2$ teaspoon oregano
    Salt and black pepper to
    taste
  1 tablespoon parsley
  1 bouquet garni*

EQUIPMENT
Large skillet

In a large skillet, heat the olive oil. Sauté the onion and garlic in the hot oil until the onion is browned. Add the mushrooms and cook for a minute in the oil, stirring continuously. Stir in the chopped tomatoes, white wine, oregano, salt, and black pepper; add the bouquet garni to the skillet. Simmer gently for 15 minutes, stirring occasionally. Remove and discard the bouquet garni, sprinkle the mushrooms with chopped parsley, and serve immediately. Makes 4 side-dish servings.

  *A bouquet garni consists of fresh parsley, thyme, and bay leaves (and occasionally celery) that you tie together with a string and use to infuse a dish with flavor and aroma while cooking. It is removed and discarded before serving.

Did you know . . . ?

  🍎 George Harrison is, of course, a brilliant guitarist. But did you know that he is also an accomplished bass player? In fact, George played bass on several of the Beatles' most memorable recordings, including "Back in the U.S.S.R.," "Rocky Raccoon," "Honey Pie," "Birthday," and "She Came In Through the Bathroom Window." (Guess Paul was busy, eh?)

*You'll fall for Savory Truffles
(even if they're really mushrooms).
(Photo courtesy of Photofest)*

Wild Potato Pie

("Wild Honey Pie")

This really wacky pie is a tribute to that really wacky *White Album* song!

INGREDIENTS
- 5 large Idaho potatoes, diced, parboiled (approximately 8 to 12 minutes, depending on size of potatoes—do not fully cook), and drained
- ¼ cup (½ stick) salted butter
- 4 ounces (115 g) pepperoni, cut into small cubes (stick pepperoni works best; if not available, use sliced pepperoni cut into small pieces)
- 2 medium eggs
- 4 ounces (115 g) provolone cheese, cubed (cheddar or Muenster can be substituted if desired)
- ¼ cup (70 ml) grated Parmesan cheese
- Black pepper

EQUIPMENT
Large mixing bowl
Potato masher
Pie tin

Preheat the oven to 350° F (177° C). In a large mixing bowl, combine the potatoes, butter, pepperoni, eggs, provolone, and grated Parmesan, using a potato masher to mix well. Pour the mixture into a pie tin and bake for 30 to 40 minutes, until the top is lightly browned. Let stand a short time before slicing. Serve slices as a side dish. Serves 6 to 8.

Ticket to Rice

("Ticket to Ride")

This fast, tasty (and very simple!) tomato and cheese risotto dish will really satisfy you so you can hit the road with your ticket to ride.

INGREDIENTS
- 1 19-ounce (565 ml) can Progresso tomato soup
- 2 cups (550 ml) Minute Rice
- 1 or 2 slices sharp cheddar cheese

EQUIPMENT
Large glass microwave-safe bowl
Flat serving dish

In a large glass bowl, combine the tomato soup and Minute Rice. Mix well. Cover with plastic wrap or paper towel and microwave on high for 8 to 8$^1/_2$ minutes, turning every 2 minutes if your microwave does not have a rotating turntable. Remove from the microwave and mix well. Spoon the risotto out onto a flat dish and cover with 1 or 2 slices of cheddar cheese. Allow the cheese to melt. Serve with a garden salad and French bread. Serves 4.

"Quick, lads, before they eat all the Run for Your Rice!"
(Photo courtesy of Photofest; Copyright © 1975 United Artists Corporation)

Run for Your Rice
("Run for Your Life")

Maybe John wouldn't have been so jealous in "Run for Your Life" if he'd had a big bowl of this delicious rice dish to keep him busy, eh?

INGREDIENTS

3 cups (825 ml) cold cooked rice

$^1/_4$ cup (70 ml) chopped pimientos

$^1/_2$ cup (140 ml) chopped green pepper

$^3/_4$ cup (210 ml) chopped celery

$^1/_4$ cup (70 ml) green olives stuffed with pimientos, sliced thin

$^1/_4$ cup (70 ml) fine-chopped onion

$^1/_2$ teaspoon salt

Black pepper to taste

$^1/_4$ cup (60 ml) French dressing

$^1/_2$ cup (120 ml) mayonnaise

EQUIPMENT

Large mixing bowl

Small mixing bowl

In a large mixing bowl, combine the rice, pimientos, green pepper, celery, olives, onion, salt, and black pepper to taste and toss lightly. In a small bowl, blend the French dressing and mayonnaise. Pour the dressing over the rice and vegetables and mix until well blended. Serve as a side dish. Serves 6.

Did you know . . . ?

🍎 John took the opening line of "Run for Your Life"—"I'd rather see you dead, little girl, than to be with another man"—from an old Elvis Presley recording called "Baby, Let's Play House." John never liked "Run for Your Life" and admitted that he wrote it simply because the Beatles needed one more song for the *Rubber Soul* album.

I Saw Her String Beans There!

("I Saw Her Standing There")

In honor of the incredible creativity manifested on a regular basis by the Beatles, this recipe will not include amounts! Why? Because this tasty delight was invented by me wife, Pam, and she never measures when she makes it. You'll just have to be as creative as she is when putting this fab vegetable dish together! Don't worry, though: The instructions will be specific enough so you'll be sure to end up with Polythene Pam's delicious string beans (which are known around the Spignesi compound as String Beans à la Pam).

INGREDIENTS
- 2 16-ounce (450 g each) cans French-cut string beans (salt-free is okay)
- Olive oil (a bold, extra-virgin oil will yield the best results)
- Italian-flavored bread crumbs
- Garlic salt (garlic powder is okay)

EQUIPMENT
- Large mixing bowl
- Large saucepan or large oven baking dish

Drain the 2 cans of string beans and place them in a large mixing bowl. Add olive oil until the beans are moist (but not dripping wet). Add some bread crumbs and combine until the mixture gets pasty. Add more olive oil and more bread crumbs until the mixture reaches a nice, thick consistency. (A spoonful of it held upside down should not fall off the spoon.) Sprinkle a good amount (at least 1 or 2 tablespoons to start) of garlic salt or powder on the mixture and combine well. Add more if you like a real garlicky flavor. Now decide if you want to heat it on top of the stove or in the oven. (Either works fine.) If on top of the stove, heat the mixture in an uncovered pan over medium heat until nice and hot. (When it starts to get warm, taste it and add more garlic powder or garlic salt if you like.) If you heat it in the oven, bake at 350° F (177° C) uncovered, until hot. You can also add black pepper to taste if you like.

VARIATIONS ON A STRING BEAN

You can add many ingredients to this recipe to enhance it (although you really should try it unadorned at least once before you start improvising). Chopped black olives are good, as are french-fried onions (the canned ones: When the crispy onions heat up and combine with the olive oil, they get soft and add a lot of flavor). Chopped mushrooms are nice, too, and you can even add a heaping handful of a shredded cheese of your choice before heating for a very hearty (albeit stringy!) main dish. If you'd like to try one of these variations, add your "extras" to the string bean mixture (combine well) just before heating.

SERVING SUGGESTIONS

I Saw Her String Beans There! can be served and eaten in many ways. You can spoon it out and eat it as a vegetable side dish with any main course—including pasta dishes. You can place a flat layer of it in a dish, cover it with sliced provolone, mozzarella, Muenster, cheddar, or Swiss cheese, and eat it as a main dish with a crusty bread. You can spoon it into an Italian bread grinder (a.k.a. hero or submarine—sub—sandwich), sprinkle with grated cheese (or cover with a sliced cheese of your choice), and eat it as the tastiest vegetable burger grinder you've ever tried! (In a sandwich is my personal favorite . . . although you do need to make sure the final consistency of the string beans and bread crumbs is *really thick* in order for it to work this way.)

Did you know . . . ?

- Originally, Paul's opening lyrics for "I Saw Her Standing There" were, "Well, she was just seventeen/Never been a beauty queen." John hated the "beauty queen" line and insisted Paul change it to the *much* better "Well, she was just seventeen/You know what I mean."

Inspired by a bowl of Michelle's Mashed Potatoes, Paul composes a lovely ode to that fictitious French girl. (Photo courtesy of Photofest)

Michelle's Mashed Potatoes

("Michelle")

Potatoes, butter, Parmesan cheese, and oregano: These are things that go together well! Mmm!

INGREDIENTS

2¹/₂ pounds (1.1 kg) baking potatoes, washed and peeled

2¹/₂ tablespoons salted butter

1¹/₄ cups (345 ml) freshly grated Parmesan cheese

¹/₄ cup (60 ml) warm milk

¹/₄ teaspoon salt

1 teaspoon oregano

EQUIPMENT

Large pot with cover

Colander

Potato masher

Cut the potatoes into 1-inch (25 mm) slices. Fill a large pot approximately three-quarters full with water. Place the potatoes in the pot and bring to a rolling boil over high heat. When the pot reaches the rolling boil, cover, reduce the heat, and continue cooking for 17 minutes more. Remove the pot from the heat and thoroughly drain the potatoes in a colander. Place the potatoes back in the pot. Using the potato masher, mash the potatoes until they are smooth. Return the pot to the stove and place it over low heat. Add to the potatoes the butter, Parmesan cheese, milk, salt, and oregano. Continue mashing the potatoes until they are again smooth. (You can add small amounts of milk while mashing to soften the consistency if desired.) Serve immediately. Serves 4.

Did you know . . . ?

● There was no real Michelle—Paul had been listening to a Nina Simone record and just ended up feeling like writing something with a "French" feel to it. Thus, a classic was born.

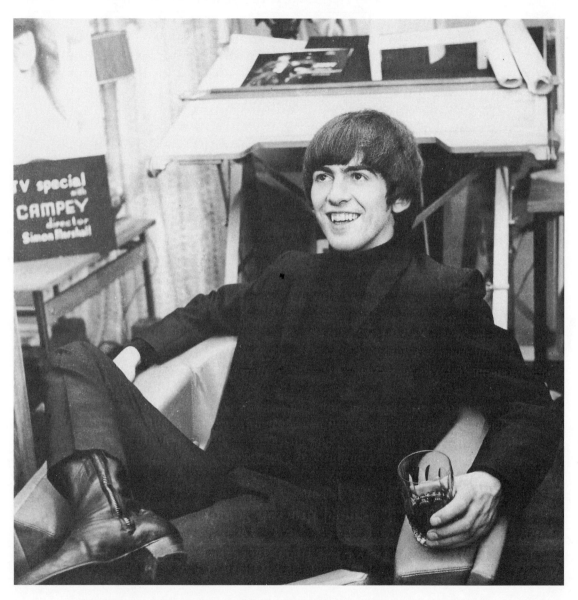

Kicking back with a delicious Beatle beverage. (Photo courtesy of Photofest)

Beatle
Beverages

"Who ordered the bubbly? It better not be on me tab!"
(Photo courtesy of Photofest; Copyright © Official Beatles Fan Club)

Good Day Champagne

("Good Day Sunshine")

Even though it will, indeed, be a "good day" when you imbibe this delicious brew, it takes a good four weeks to ferment, so plan ahead!

INGREDIENTS
- 7 medium, all-purpose potatoes
- 7 oranges
- 7 lemons
- 7 pounds (3.18 kg) sugar
- 7 quarts (6.65 l) water
- 1 pound (450 g) raisins, ground

- 1 package ($^1/_4$ ounce/8g) dry yeast
- 1 slice toast

EQUIPMENT
Large covered crock
Wooden spoon
Mesh strainer

Peel and slice the potatoes, oranges, and lemons 1/8 to 1/4 inch (3 to 6 mm) thick. Place in a large crock and add the sugar, water, and raisins. Mix well with a wooden spoon. Place the yeast on top of the slice of toast and place the toast on top of the water in the crock. Remove the toast after 1 week. Let the mixture set for 2 weeks and then strain through a mesh strainer. Let the mixture set for 3 days and strain again. Let the mixture set for 3 more days, strain one last time, and bottle. Makes almost 2 gallons (8 l).

Hey Juice

("Hey Jude")

This delicious fruit juice float will get under your skin, if you let it into your heart!

INGREDIENTS
½ *cup (120 ml) lemon sherbet*
¾ *cup (180 ml) orange juice*

EQUIPMENT
12-ounce (355 ml) glass

Add half of the sherbet to the chilled glass. Add enough of the orange juice to fill the glass halfway. Stir gently. Add the remaining sherbet. Fill to the brim with the remaining orange juice. Serves 1.

VARIATIONS ON A FLOAT
Any flavor of sherbet or ice cream can be substituted for the lemon sherbet. (Watermelon sherbet makes for an especially tasty float!) Also, apple, grape, or pineapple juice can be substituted for the orange juice in this recipe. Experiment with the flavors, because, after all, the moment you need is on your shoulder!

Did you know . . . ?

- "Hey Jude" is the Beatles' longest single at seven minutes and nine seconds, although it would only be a little over three minutes long if the chanting "Na, na, na, na, hey Jude" ending was eliminated. (But who would want *that,* eh?)

Billy Shears's Sherry Surprise

(Sgt. Pepper's Lonely Hearts Club Band)

This *Sgt. Pepper*–inspired drink may be hard to say, but it sure does go down easy.

INGREDIENTS

$^{1}/_{2}$ cup (120 ml) semidry sherry
1 tablespoon bottled orange syrup
    Juice of 1 large lemon
    Chopped ice
1 teaspoon bottled strawberry syrup
1 tablespoon port wine

3 cups (710 ml) unflavored seltzer
4 orange slices ($^{1}/_{8}$-inch/ 3 mm thick)

EQUIPMENT

Large cocktail shaker
4 tall glasses

Place the sherry, orange syrup, and lemon juice in a large cocktail shaker and fill almost to the top with chopped ice. Shake well. Add the strawberry syrup and port to the cocktail shaker and stir. Pour the contents of the shaker, divided equally, into 4 tall glasses. Fill each glass to the top with seltzer and garnish with a slice of orange. Makes 4 8-ounce (235 ml) drinks.

Did you know . . . ?

🍎 *Sgt. Pepper's Lonely Hearts Club Band* was originally supposed to be titled *Dr. Pepper's Lonely Hearts Club Band*—until the boys found out about a certain American soft-drink company that had a rather proprietary interest in the name "Dr. Pepper"!

Multicolored Milk Shake

("Happiness Is a Warm Gun")

This sweet and delicious milk shake is so good those taste buds'll be "busy working overtime"!

INGREDIENTS
- 1 pint (475 ml) vanilla/chocolate/strawberry ice cream (or ⅓ pint/155 ml of each individual flavor)
- ¾ cup (180 ml) milk
- 1½ ounces (45 g; approximately 1 single-serving bag) plain M & M candy

EQUIPMENT
Blender

Place the ice cream and milk in a blender, cover, and blend until mixture is smooth. Add the M & Ms, cover, and blend until the candy is coarsely chopped. Serve immediately. Makes 2 8-ounce (235 ml) servings.

Ringo's Drum Rum Punch

(In Honor of Ringo Starr)

Because Ringo has quit drinking, his batch will have to be *sans* rum. You can make yours "hard," though.

INGREDIENTS
- 1 12-ounce (355 ml) can frozen fruit juice concentrate, partially thawed
- 2 cups (475 ml) water
- 1 cup (235 ml) unsweetened pineapple juice
- 2 12-ounce (355 ml each) bottles Sprite
- 1 cup (235 ml) light rum (more to taste)
- Ice cubes

EQUIPMENT
Large pitcher

A classic shot of Ringo at the drums. (Photo courtesy of Photofest)

Combine the fruit juice concentrate, water, and pineapple juice in a large pitcher and stir until completely liquefied. Slowly stir in 2 bottles of Sprite. Add rum, ice cubes, and stir. Makes 18 4-ounce (120 ml) servings.

Did you know . . . ?

🖤 The titles of the Beatles songs "A Hard Day's Night," "Eight Days a Week," and "Tomorrow Never Knows" all came about thanks to Ringo's penchant for wonderful malapropisms.

I'm Only Steeping

("I'm Only Sleeping")

Since tea seems to be the national beverage in the United Kingdom, this smooth no-boil iced tea recipe is the perfect accompaniment for a nice leisurely afternoon spent listening to *Revolver*. (Just don't fall asleep while you're waiting for this sun tea to brew!)

INGREDIENTS
  8 tea bags of your choice
1¹/₂ quarts (1.4 l) cold water

EQUIPMENT
*2-quart (1.9 l) clear glass
  container*

Place the tea bags in the glass container. Add cold water and cover tightly. Place the container in the direct sun for 2 to 3 hours, or until the tea is the strength you like it. (If it's a cloudy day, letting the tea steep at room temperature will also work, but it comes out better if it steeps in the sun.) Serve over ice with sugar and lemon if desired. Makes 6 8-ounce (235 ml) servings.

Stupid Bloody Mary

("I Am the Walrus")

This delicious beverage serves as the perfect icebreaker when "we are all together."

INGREDIENTS

1 32-ounce (950 ml) bottle tomato juice
8 ounces (235 ml) vodka
1/4 cup (60 ml) lemon juice
2 teaspoons Worcestershire sauce
1/4 teaspoon celery salt
4 dashes bottled hot pepper sauce (more or less to taste)
Ice cubes
10 celery stalks

EQUIPMENT
Large pitcher

In a large pitcher, combine the tomato juice, vodka, lemon juice, Worcestershire sauce, celery salt, and hot pepper sauce; stir well. Pour into 6-ounce (180 ml) glasses over ice cubes and serve with a celery stalk. Makes 10 drinks of a little over 4 ounces (120 ml) each.

Velvet Hand

("Happiness Is a Warm Gun")

Happiness may be a warm gun, but this delightful beverage will acquaint you with the touch of champagne and brandy's velvet hand—and you can hold the lizard!

INGREDIENTS

4 ounces (120 ml) champagne
1 ounce (30 ml) peach brandy
Canned peach slices
Cracked ice

EQUIPMENT
8-ounce (235 ml) tumbler

Place a couple of peach slices in the bottom of the tumbler. Add some cracked ice. Add the champagne, then the peach brandy, and stir gently. Makes 1 smooth drink.

Did you know . . . ?

 John Lennon's life was an exercise in irony: He was born during a World War II air raid, he died a victim of gun violence, and yet he spent his entire artistic life preaching . . . peace.

(Photo courtesy of author's collection)

A Beatles Magical Mystery Puzzle

Unscramble the fourteen Beatles song titles and keep track of the double-under-lined letter in each answer. When you decipher all the mixed-up titles, the four-teen double-underlined letters will spell out the title of ... let's call it "little-known" Beatles album, but one that will fit right in with everything else in *She Came In Through the Kitchen Window*. Roll up!

1. UHWEIALMTARS
   — —= — — — — — — — — —

2. VADEILROHNE
   — — — — — — — — —=—

3. OAILNLMYLVG
   =— — — — — — — — — —

4. TITOICETRKDE
   — — — — — —=— — — — —

5. TEKERELSHTREL
   — — — — — — — — — —=— —

6. THEMLEWLY
   — — — — — — —=—

7. MEDLVEOO
   — — —= — — — —

8. KLARBCBID
   — — — — —=— —

9. UDDERCERPANE
   — — — — — — — — — —=

10. DERYCIVMAR
    — — — — — — — — —=—

11. DYOTOHOUNTRHAIWALND
    — — — —= — — — — — — — — — — — — —

12. LWILI
    — — —=—

13. EDETNH
    — —= — — —

14. DSEAIYXSE
    =— — — — — — —

(Solution on page 215)

(Photo courtesy of Photofest)

"#9 Dream"
Desserts and
Snacks

Ringo had to be restrained from eating all of the Can't Buy Me Fudge—even after he had burst his trousers. (Photo courtesy of Photofest)

Can't Buy Me Fudge

("Can't Buy Me Love")

As we learned from Paul and John's lyrics in "Can't Buy Me Love," money can't buy us love . . . but it sure can buy some terrific, nutty fudge.

INGREDIENTS
- ¹/₂ cup (1 stick) salted butter
- 1 cup (275 ml) packed brown sugar
- ¹/₄ cup (60 ml) milk
- 2 cups (550 ml) sifted confectioners' sugar
- 1 cup (275 ml) cashews

EQUIPMENT
- 9 × 9 inch (23 × 23 cm) pan
- Medium saucepan

Grease the baking pan. In a medium saucepan, melt the butter and add the brown sugar. Cook the butter-and-sugar mixture over low heat for 2 minutes, stirring constantly. Add the milk to the mixture and continue cooking until it all comes to a boil. Remove the pan from the heat and let it cool. Once the mixture has cooled, slowly add the confectioners' sugar, stirring continuously until the mixture is the consistency of fudge. Add the nuts and mix gently. Spread the fudge in the greased pan and cool. Makes 36 1/2-inch (13 mm) square pieces.

Strawberries in a Field Forever

("Strawberry Fields Forever")

Let me take you down . . . to the grocery store to buy the ingredients for this fabulous and unique dessert. You won't be disappointed! (Contributed by Cheryl Tucker.)

INGREDIENTS
30 very large strawberries, stems removed
1 tablespoon water
1 tablespoon unsalted butter, melted
3 tablespoons sugar

Vanilla ice cream or strawberry sorbet (optional)

EQUIPMENT
Large baking dish
Pastry brush

Preheat the oven to 400° F (205° C). Place the strawberries, side by side and stem-end down, in a baking dish. Add the water to the dish. Brush the berries with the melted butter and sprinkle with the sugar. Bake for 6 to 8 minutes, until the berries are soft. Serve warm with the pan juices, with or without strawberry sorbet or vanilla ice cream. Serves 5.

Ringo and Barbara's wedding would have been even more special if they had served Strawberry Fields Shortcake. (Photo courtesy of Photofest)

It Won't Be Long Pie

("It Won't Be Long")

This delicious no-bake pie (that doesn't take long at all to prepare) is the perfect dessert for days when you don't have "any time at all."

INGREDIENTS
- 1 3.4-ounce (96 g) package banana instant pudding
- 1 8-ounce (225 g) can crushed pineapple
- 1 tablespoon sugar
- 1 pound (450 g) sour cream

EQUIPMENT
Large mixing bowl
Electric beater
1 9-inch (23 cm) ready-made round piecrust

In a large mixing bowl, mix all the ingredients with an electric beater on low for 1 minute. Pour the mixture into the piecrust and chill for 3 hours or more. Serves 8.

Ginger Sling Pie

("Savoy Truffle")

This unique no-bake ginger ale and pear pie will satisfy your sweet tooth when you can't get your hands on a ginger sling with a pineapple heart.

INGREDIENTS
1¼ cups (295 ml) ginger ale
- 1 3.4-ounce (96 g) package lime Jell-O
- 1 pint (475 ml) vanilla ice cream
- 1 20-ounce (565 g) can pears, drained and diced
- 1 9-inch (23 cm) cooked piecrust

EQUIPMENT
Large saucepan

Heat the ginger ale in a large saucepan until it is almost boiling, then add the package of lime Jell-O. Lower the heat and stir continuously until the Jell-O completely dissolves. Add 1 pint of vanilla ice cream to the pan and blend it into the liquid thoroughly on low heat. Remove the pan from the heat and let cool until the filling begins to set. Mix the diced pears into the pie filling and then spoon the mixture into the piecrust. Chill and serve with whipped cream. Serves 8.

Did you know . . . ?

🍎 George Harrison's father, Harold, was once a ballroom dancing instructor.

Yellow Matter Custard

("I Am the Walrus")

If you can get past the less-than-tasteful lyrical reference in the title of this recipe and in the song itself, you will really enjoy this tasty dessert!

INGREDIENTS
3 medium eggs, beaten
1¹/₂ cups (355 ml) milk
¹/₃ cup (90 g) sugar
1 teaspoon vanilla extract
¹/₂ banana, mashed
Cinnamon

EQUIPMENT
Mixing bowl
4 6-ounce (180 ml) custard
cups
8 × 8 inch (20 × 20 cm)
baking dish

Preheat the oven to 325° F (163° C). Combine eggs, milk, sugar, vanilla, and mashed banana in mixing bowl. Beat together until well blended but not foamy. Place the custard cups in the baking dish. Pour custard mixture into the cups. Sprinkle the tops with ground cinnamon. Pour boiling water into the baking dish around the custard cups to a depth of 1 inch (25 mm). Bake the custard for between 30 and 45 minutes: Test by inserting a knife blade into the center. When the knife comes out clean, the custard is done. Serve warm or chilled. Serves 4.

I Wanna Be Your Flan

("I Wanna Be Your Man")

Paul and John originally wrote "I Wanna Be Your Man" for the Rolling Stones. In the September 1980 *Playboy,* a few months before he died, John disparaged the tune by pointing out that the only two versions of the song (other than the Beatles' live-concert version) were by Ringo and the Stones. "That shows how much importance we put on it."

This "I Wanna Be Your Flan," however, will find an important place in your recipe repertoire once you try it.

INGREDIENTS
⅔ cup (185 ml) sugar
3 medium eggs, beaten
1½ cups (355 ml) milk
1 teaspoon vanilla extract
Cinnamon

EQUIPMENT
Heavy saucepan
Mixing bowl
4 6-ounce (180 ml) custard cups
8 × 8 inch (21 × 21 cm)
  baking dish

Preheat the oven to 325° F (163° C). Cook half the sugar in a heavy saucepan over medium-high heat until the sugar begins to melt. Reduce the heat and continue cooking until the sugar is golden brown. Divide this cooked sugar evenly into each of the custard cups, being sure to coat the bottoms of the cups. Combine the eggs, milk, the rest of the sugar, and vanilla in a mixing bowl. Beat together until well blended but not foamy. Place the custard cups in the baking dish. Pour the custard mixture into the cups on top of the cooked sugar. Sprinkle the tops with ground cinnamon. Pour boiling water into the baking dish around the custard cups to a depth of 1 inch (25 mm). Bake the flan for between 30 and 45 minutes. Test the flan by inserting a knife blade into the center. When it comes out clean, the flan is done. Remove the flan from the custard cups to serve. (Inverting the flan so the cooked sugar is on top makes for a nice presentation.) Serves 4.

A Taste of Honey

("A Taste of Honey")

"A Taste of Honey" appeared on the early Beatles album *Please Please Me* and was part of the Fabs' live repertoire for many years, even though it was not written by John and Paul. Originally composed for the 1960 play *A Taste of Honey,* the song was given a nice treatment by the Beatles, but it was made more popular by Herb Alpert and the Tijuana Brass with their very successful 1965 instrumental version. These delicious "Taste of Honey" fried dough balls are based on an old Italian recipe that has been in my family for years; we usually make them for the Easter and Christmas holidays.

INGREDIENTS

$^1/_2$ cup (140 ml) sugar
2 medium eggs
1 cup (275 ml) all-purpose
   flour
   Corn oil for deep-frying
   Honey to taste

EQUIPMENT

Large mixing bowl
Large skillet
Slotted spoon
Large cookie sheet

In a large mixing bowl, beat together the sugar and eggs. Add the flour and mix well until it forms a thick batter. Heat the corn oil in a large skillet until hot (use enough oil to submerge the balls, i.e. approximately 1/2 to 1 inch deep). Cut the batter into marble-sized balls (it is easier if you roll the dough out long and thin first). Fry the balls in the hot oil until they are golden brown. Remove the cooked balls from the oil with a slotted spoon, draining off the oil. Place on a flat cookie sheet and pour honey on top of the balls, covering them completely. Allow them to cool and harden. Serve as a snack. Makes 36 to 48 honey balls.

Devil Dogs in Her Heart

("Devil in Her Heart")

Even though they didn't write it, "Devil in Her Heart" was a very popular part of the Beatles' live-concert playlist in 1962 and 1963.

Their name notwithstanding, these delicious chocolaty cookies will be sure to have everyone calling *you* an angel!

INGREDIENTS

COOKIES

*1/2 cup (140 ml) vegetable
  shortening*
1/2 cup (140 ml) dark cocoa
1 cup (275 ml) sugar
1 cup (235 ml) milk
1 medium egg
*2 cups (550 ml) all-purpose
  flour*
1/2 teaspoon baking powder
1/2 teaspoon salt
1/2 teaspoon baking soda
1 teaspoon vanilla extract

FILLING

*3/4 cup (210 ml) vegetable
  shortening*
*1 2/3 cups (460 ml)
  confectioners' sugar*
1/2 teaspoon vanilla extract
*7 ounces (205 ml)
  Marshmallow Fluff*

EQUIPMENT

Large mixing bowl
Ungreased cookie sheet

Preheat the oven to 400° F (205° C). *Make the cookies:* In a large mixing bowl, mix the vegetable shortening, dark cocoa, and sugar. Add to this mixture the milk, egg, flour, baking powder, salt, baking soda, and vanilla. Drop teaspoons of this batter onto an ungreased cookie sheet and bake for 8 minutes.

While the cookies are baking, make the filling by mixing together the vegetable shortening, confectioners' sugar, vanilla, and Marshmallow Fluff. Mix well, adding a little milk to make the mixture thin enough to spread on the cookies. When the cookies have cooled, spread the filling mixture evenly on one cookie and use a second cookie for the top. Makes 12 (or so) cookies.

Sweet Georgia Brownies

("Sweet Georgia Brown")

"Sweet Georgia Brown" was one of the classic covers the Beatles did in their early days together. The song was actually released in the United States in June 1964 as a single (with a B side of "Take Out Some Insurance on Me, Baby").

This classic brownie recipe is dedicated to the memory of all those classic R&B and rock 'n' roll songs the Beatles performed in the hungry years.

INGREDIENTS
- $^1/_2$ cup (120 ml) melted salted butter
- 2 cups (550 ml) packed dark brown sugar
- 2 medium eggs
- $^1/_2$ teaspoon salt
- $1^1/_2$ cups (415 ml) all-purpose flour
- 2 teaspoons baking powder
- 1 teaspoon vanilla extract
- 1 cup (275 ml) semisweet chocolate chips

EQUIPMENT
Large mixing bowl
9 × 12 inch (23 × 30 cm) cake pan

Preheat the oven to 350° F (177° C). In a large bowl, mix together all the ingredients, adding the chocolate chips last. Mix well. Butter the baking pan. Spread out the brownie batter in the pan and bake for 25 to 30 minutes. When cooked, the top of the brownie should be dry and springy to the touch. Let cool for 15 minutes and then cut into 36 small squares.

George's Crackerbox Palace Icebox Cake

("Crackerbox Palace")

In 1988 George Harrison said, "I think you have to just make something that you enjoy yourself and see what happens." Me mum, Lee, invented this scrumptious Icebox Cake and, since she really enjoyed it, she took to heart George's philosophy and christened her recipe to honor one of her favorite Harrisongs.

INGREDIENTS

2 3.4-ounce (96 g each) packages chocolate pudding
2 3.4-ounce (96 g each) packages vanilla pudding
8 cups (1.9 l) milk (for puddings)
1¹/₂ 16-ounce (450 g each) boxes cinnamon graham crackers

3 ripe bananas, sliced approximately ¹/₄ inch (6 mm) thick
Cinnamon

EQUIPMENT

2 medium saucepans
9 × 12 inch (23 × 30 cm) glass dish
Aluminum foil

In separate pans, cook the chocolate and vanilla puddings according to package directions. Remove from the heat and allow both pans to cool.

Line the bottom of the glass dish with enough cinnamon graham crackers to completely cover the bottom. (Break pieces of crackers to the appropriate size if necessary.) Spoon a layer of chocolate pudding on top of the graham crackers. Lay banana slices on top of the chocolate pudding until the pudding is completely covered. Crumble 1 or 2 graham crackers by hand and sprinkle the crumbs on top of the banana slices. Place another layer of graham crackers on top of the bananas, completely covering the slices. Spoon a layer of vanilla pudding on top of the graham crackers. Lay banana slices on top of the vanilla pudding until the pudding is completely covered. Sprinkle more graham cracker crumbs on top of the bananas. Place another layer of graham crackers on top of the bananas, completely covering the slices. Spoon vanilla pudding on one half of the graham crackers; spoon chocolate pudding on the other half. Lay banana slices on top of the vanilla and chocolate puddings until they're completely covered. Sprinkle more graham cracker crumbs and a light dusting of cinnamon on top of the bananas.

Cover the dish with aluminum foil and refrigerate for at least 2 to 4 hours. (This should be eaten cold.) Serves 10.

Abbey Roll

(Abbey Road)

There's a rumor going around that the real reason the Beatles were crossing Abbey Road was that this incredible chocolate rum roll was on the other side!

INGREDIENTS
- 7 medium eggs
- 1 cup (275 ml) sugar
- ¹/₂ pound (225 g) dark sweet chocolate
- 7 tablespoons ground coffee
  Pinch salt
  Nonstick vegetable cooking spray
  Bitter cocoa powder
- 2 cups (475 ml) heavy cream, whipped
- 2 tablespoons rum

EQUIPMENT
Small mixing bowl
Large mixing bowl
Small saucepan
Jelly roll pan
Wax paper
Kitchen dishtowel

Separate the 7 eggs. Place the yolks in a small mixing bowl and the whites in a large mixing bowl. Add the sugar to the yolks and beat until the mixture is light, fluffy, and creamy. Set aside.

In a small saucepan, melt together the dark sweet chocolate and coffee over *very low* heat. When this is melted, allow it to cool slightly. While the chocolate is cooling, beat the egg whites with a pinch of salt until stiff. Preheat the oven to 350° F (177° C). Fold the egg yolks and the melted chocolate into the beaten egg whites.

Spray a jelly roll pan with vegetable cooking spray, cover with wax paper, and spray the wax paper with vegetable cooking spray. Spread the chocolate mixture into the pan and bake for 15 to 20 minutes. Remove from the oven and let cool for 5 minutes.

Cover the cake with a slightly damp cloth (a clean dishtowel works beautifully) and allow it to cool completely at room temperature. When completely cooled, refrigerate the cake in its pan for 1 hour. Remove the cloth carefully and sprinkle the top of the cake with bitter cocoa. Carefully turn the baked cake out onto wax paper so that the wax paper that was underneath the cake is now on top. Discard the wax paper that is now on top of the cake. Mix the whipped heavy cream with the rum. Spread this mixture evenly on top of the cake. Very carefully roll up the cake like a jelly roll. It will crack as it is rolled, and resemble the bark of a tree when completed. Serves 6 to 8.

Did you know . . . ?

🍎 According to Paul McCartney, the *Abbey Road* album was originally going to be titled *Everest*, in honor of recording engineer Geoff Emerick's favorite cigarettes. The Beatles also actually considered flying to Mount Everest and having their picture taken on its foothills for the album cover. One wonders what "Paul Is Dead" clues such a photo would have inspired!

Apple Braid

(Apple Corps)

Apple was the Beatles' dream company, a company formed to promote art for art's sake; a company to which struggling artists could come to make their records and films without having to toe the corporate line. Mismanagement ultimately doomed it, but the Fabs' intentions were admirable.

To honor the noble vision of Apple, here is a wonderful apple pastry to indulge in!

INGREDIENTS

Butter-flavored nonstick
vegetable cooking spray
1 8-ounce (225 g) package
refrigerated crescent rolls
2 tablespoons all-purpose flour
$^{1}/_{3}$ cup (90 ml) granulated sugar
$^{1}/_{4}$ teaspoon cinnamon
$^{1}/_{8}$ teaspoon ground nutmeg
$^{1}/_{8}$ teaspoon ground cloves
2 medium Granny Smith
apples, peeled, cored, and
cut into quarters

2 tablespoons ($^{1}/_{4}$ stick)
salted butter
$^{1}/_{4}$ cup (70 ml) confectioners'
sugar
1 tablespoon milk

EQUIPMENT

9×12 inch (23×30 cm) baking
sheet
Large mixing bowl
Small saucepan

Preheat the oven to 375° F (190° C). Spray baking sheet with butter-flavored vegetable cooking spray. Unroll crescent dough and place it on the baking sheet. Roll the dough flat to seal the perforations. Sprinkle the dough with flour. In a large mixing bowl, combine granulated sugar, cinnamon, nutmeg, and cloves. Add the apples and mix well so the apples get coated with the spices. Place the apple mixture in the middle of the dough in a strip about 2 inches (5 cm) wide. Cut 10 slits in the dough about $^{3}/_{4}$ inch (19 mm) wide on each side of the apple mixture. Braid each strip over the top of the apples at an angle, alternating from side to side. Fold the ends of the dough to seal the braid.

In a small saucepan, melt the butter. Brush the melted butter over the top of the braid. Bake for 30 minutes. Just before the braid is finished baking, combine the confectioners' sugar and milk, stirring until smooth. Pour this glaze over the warm Apple Braid before slicing. Serves 4 to 6.

Did you know . . . ?

 During the Beatles' final live performance as a group, on the roof of the Apple building in London on January 30, 1969, John Lennon was wearing a woman's fur jacket.

Sundae's on the Phone to Monday

("She Came In Through the Bathroom Window")

This delightful banana split sundae with its fresh-made toppings takes a little extra effort, but it's worth the time. The result is so delicious that you'll be on the phone till Monday telling all your friends about it!

HOT FUDGE SAUCE

INGREDIENTS
³/₄ cup (210 ml) semisweet chocolate pieces
¹/₄ cup (¹/₂ stick) salted butter
²/₃ cup (185 ml) sugar

1 5-ounce (140 ml) can evaporated milk

EQUIPMENT
Small heavy saucepan

In a small saucepan, melt together the chocolate pieces and butter. Add the sugar. Gradually stir in the evaporated milk. Bring to a boil and reduce the heat. Boil for 8 minutes over a low heat, stirring often. Remove from the heat. Makes 1¹/₂ cups (355 ml).

FRUIT SAUCE

INGREDIENTS

$^1/_2$ teaspoon fine-shredded
   orange peel
$^1/_4$ cup (60 ml) orange juice
1 tablespoon cornstarch
$^1/_4$ teaspoon cinnamon

1 8-ounce (225 g) can fruit
   cocktail with juice

EQUIPMENT
Small heavy saucepan

In a small saucepan, mix the orange peel, orange juice, cornstarch, and cinnamon. Stir in the fruit cocktail with its juice. Cook and stir until the mixture begins to bubble. Cook and stir for 2 more minutes. Makes $1^1/_3$ cups (320 ml).

THE SUNDAE'S ON THE PHONE TO MONDAY SUNDAE

INGREDIENTS

1 large ripe banana
3 scoops ice cream of choice
1 scoop Marshmallow Fluff
1 scoop Hot Fudge Sauce
1 scoop Fruit Sauce

Whipped cream
Chopped nuts of choice
3 maraschino cherries

EQUIPMENT
1 long dessert dish

Cut the banana in half lengthwise and place in a long dessert dish. Plop the 3 scoops of ice cream down its length. Top one of the scoops with the Marshmallow Fluff; top another scoop with the Hot Fudge Sauce; top the third scoop with the Fruit Sauce. Squirt whipped cream on top of all 3 mounds of ice cream, top with nuts, and place 1 maraschino cherry atop each mound. Serves 1.

John Lennon and the Number "9"

John Lennon always believed that the number 9 had great significance and played an important role in his life. He assigned talismanic gravity to its appearance in his life and also deliberately tried to use it in his daily activities whenever possible.

Here is a look at some of the appearances of the number 9 in John Lennon's life. (And by the way, there are 27 items of fact listed here. Now, 2 plus 7 equals 9; and 27 is also divisible by 9 precisely 3 times—which is the number of Beatles remaining after John's death. I swear to God I did not plan it that way. It just happened. Imagine that.)

- ⑨ John was born on the ninth day of the tenth month of 1940: October 9, 1940.
- ⑨ When John was young, his mother lived at 9 Newcastle Road, Wavertree, Liverpool.
- ⑨ "Newcastle" has nine letters.
- ⑨ "Wavertree" has nine letters.
- ⑨ "Liverpool" has nine letters.
- ⑨ When John was a young art student, the bus he traveled on to get to the Liverpool Art College was Bus No. 72. And 7 plus 2 equals 9.
- ⑨ Brian Epstein first saw the Beatles perform on November 9, 1961, at the Liverpool Cavern.
- ⑨ The Beatles' first record deal was secured with EMI on May 9, 1962.
- ⑨ The Beatles' first record, "Love Me Do," was released on the Parlophone label R4949.
- ⑨ During a tour in Paris in 1964 John received a letter that said, "I am going to kill you at nine tonight."
- ⑨ When John moved his aunt Mimi from Liverpool to Dorset, her address was 126 Panorama Road. And 1 plus 2 plus 6 equals 9.
- ⑨ John always used the number nine in any of the lock combinations for his many briefcases and attaché cases.

9 John's "9" songs include "Revolution No. 9," "#9 Dream," and "One After 909."

9 John first met Yoko on November 9, 1966.

9 John and Yoko lived in the Dakota, which was located on West 72nd Street in New York City. As I've noted, 7 plus 2 equals 9.

9 The first apartment John and Yoko lived in at the Dakota was apartment 72.

9 John and Yoko's album of experimental music, *Unfinished Music No. 2—Life With the Lions* was released in the United Kingdom on May 9, 1969.

9 One of the "songs" on *Unfinished Music No. 2—Life With the Lions* was "Cambridge 1969."

9 John's *Imagine* album was released in the United States on September 9, 1971.

9 John sold his Tittenhurst Park estate to Ringo on September 9, 1973.

9 John and Yoko's son Sean was born on the ninth day of the tenth month of 1975: October 9, 1975.

9 One of John's most beloved refuges in New York City was the Café La Fortuna, located at 69 West 71st Street.

9 The names "John Ono Lennon" and "Yoko Ono Lennon" combined feature the letter *o* nine times.

9 In 1979 John and Yoko published "A Love Letter From John and Yoko to People Who Ask Us What, When, and Why" in the Sunday *New York Times.* The date of the appearance of the letter was May 27. Again, 2 plus 7 equals 9. Also, the letter appeared in 1979, a year with two nines in it.

9 When John died in New York at 10:50 P.M. on December 8, 1980, the five-hour time difference meant that at the time he died, it was December 9 in Great Britain.

9 After John was shot, he was rushed to Roosevelt Hospital in New York City. Roosevelt Hospital is on Ninth Avenue.

9 The chorus of what many consider one of John's most important songs, "Give Peace a Chance," has nine words: "All we are saying is give peace a chance."

Strawberry Fields Shortcake

("Strawberry Fields Forever")

You know, I know when it's a dream . . . and this classic strawberry shortcake recipe sure fits that bill!

INGREDIENTS
- 6 cups (1.7 l) sliced fresh strawberries
- 1/2 cup (140 ml) sugar
- 2 cups (550 ml) all-purpose flour
- 2 teaspoons baking powder
- 1/2 cup (1 stick) salted butter
- 1 medium egg, beaten
- 2/3 cup (155 ml) milk
- Whipped cream

EQUIPMENT
- 8-inch (20 cm) round (1 1/2 inches/38 mm deep) baking pan
- Large mixing bowl
- Medium mixing bowl
- Small mixing bowl

Preheat the oven to 450° F (232° C). Grease the baking pan. In a large bowl, combine the strawberries and half of the sugar. Toss well and set aside. In a medium bowl, combine the remaining sugar, flour, and baking powder. Cut in the butter until the mixture resembles coarse crumbs. In a small bowl, combine the beaten egg and milk. Add this egg-and-milk mixture to the dry ingredients and stir only enough to moisten the batter. Pour the batter into the greased baking pan. Bake for 15 to 18 minutes. To test doneness, insert a toothpick into the center of the cake; when it comes out clean, the cake is done. Remove the cake from the oven and allow it to cool in its pan for 10 minutes. Remove the cake from the pan and *carefully* slice it into 2 layers. Place the bottom layer on a serving dish and spoon onto it a layer consisting of *half* of the sugared strawberries. Cover the strawberries with whipped cream and place the second cake layer on top of it. Spoon onto this layer the remaining strawberries and top with whipped cream. Serve immediately with coffee. Serves 8.

Did you know . . . ?

 John once said that "Strawberry Fields Forever" and "Help!" were the only two completely honest songs he ever wrote as a Beatle.

Marmalade Skies Pie

("Lucy in the Sky With Diamonds")

As you're eating this delightful dessert, feel free to picture yourself on a boat on a river, okay?

INGREDIENTS
- 3 cups (825 ml) all-purpose flour
- 1 tablespoon baking powder
- 3 medium eggs
- 1 cup (275 ml) sugar
- 1 teaspoon vanilla extract
- 1 6-ounce (180 ml) jar orange marmalade
- Cinnamon

EQUIPMENT
Large mixing bowls
9-inch (23 cm) pie tin

Preheat the oven to 300° F (150° C). In a large mixing bowl, mix the flour, baking powder, eggs, sugar, and vanilla. Work the dough by hand for a few minutes and then spread it out in a thin layer on the bottom of the pie tin. Reserve enough dough for the top of the pie. Spoon the orange marmalade on top of the dough until the tin is filled. Cut the remaining dough into 9-inch (23 cm) long, 1/2-inch (13 mm) wide strips. Lay the strips on top of the marmalade in a crosshatched pattern until the top is covered. Connect the ends of the dough strips to the edge of the piecrust. Sprinkle the top lightly with cinnamon. Bake for 30 to 35 minutes. Let set for several minutes before serving. Serve with vanilla ice cream. Makes 1 pie, 9 inches (23 cm) in diameter.

Did you know . . . ?

 Star Trek's William Shatner once recorded "Lucy in the Sky With Diamonds." Shatner's version is now viewed as one of the all-time worst renditions of a Beatles song ever foisted upon the listening public. (It is pretty funny, however!)

Lady (Madonna) Fingers

("Lady Madonna")

Lady Madonna herself probably couldn't have afforded to make this delicious dessert for the children at her feet (she had trouble making ends meet, you know). Still, the ingredients really aren't all that expensive, and the children at *your* feet will surely love these sweet, fruit-filled delicacies! (Contributed by Mike Lewis.)

INGREDIENTS	EQUIPMENT
³/₄ pound (3 sticks) salted butter	*Large mixing bowl*
4 cups (1,100 ml) sifted all-purpose flour	*Medium mixing bowl*
¹/₂ teaspoon baking powder	*Small mixing bowl*
2 tablespoons granulated sugar	*Rolling pin*
1 large egg's yolk	*Wax paper*
¹/₄ cup (60 ml) cold water	*Baking sheet*
2 cups (475 ml) raspberry jam	*Blender*
1 tablespoon salted butter	
1 tablespoon milk	
¹/₂ cup (140 ml) confectioners' sugar	
Vanilla extract to taste	

Rub 3/4 pound (3 sticks) of butter into the flour, baking powder, and sugar. Beat the egg yolk in water and add to the flour mixture. Mix to a stiff paste and divide into 3 equal parts. Roll 1 part very thick onto the wax paper. Prick all over with a fork, then turn over on the cookie sheet. Spread with raspberry jam. Preheat the oven to 350° F (177° C). Repeat with the other 2 parts in layers approximately measuring 8 × 12 inches (20 × 30 cm). Bake for 30 minutes. Cut into fingers, about 1 × 3 inches (2.5 × 7.5 cm) each. Blend the remaining butter and milk, then blend in the confectioners' sugar until the mixture comes to a spreading consistency. Flavor with vanilla to taste. Spread on cookies. Makes 40 cookies.

Did you know . . . ?

- Ringo once said of "Lady Madonna" that "It sounds like Elvis, doesn't it? No—no, it doesn't sound like Elvis. It *is* Elvis—even those bits where he goes very high." In what could be justifiably perceived as tacit agreement with Ringo's assessment, before he died Elvis himself recorded a cover version of "Lady Madonna."

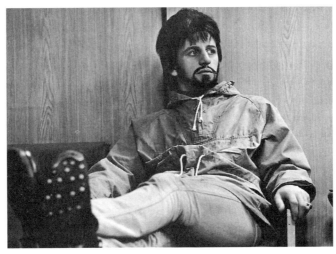

(Photo courtesy of Photofest)

Flaming Bananas (With Pie)

(Flaming Pie)

Be sure to keep a fire extinguisher nearby if you take this recipe's title to heart, okay?

INGREDIENTS

2 *ripe (but not soft) bananas*

3 *tablespoons salted butter*

3 *tablespoons brown sugar*

¹/₄ cup (60 ml) dark rum

EQUIPMENT

Medium skillet

Cut both bananas in half, then split them lengthwise. Melt the butter in a skillet over medium heat. Add the brown sugar to the butter and stir together. Add the bananas to the skillet and cook for approximately 1 minute, until they are warm and beginning to soften. Turn the bananas over and cook for an additional 30 seconds. Add the dark rum to the skillet and swirl together briefly. When the sugar, butter, and rum mixture begins to thicken slightly, remove from the heat and serve immediately. (If you choose to—and if you are *very careful*—the rum can be ignited briefly before serving, thus fulfilling the "flaming" sobriquet attached to this recipe.) Flaming Bananas can be served separately as a delicious dessert or as an accompaniment or topping for pie. (The hot, rum-flavored bananas on top of the cold, banana-flavored It Won't Be Long Pie (see page 196) is delightful; or you can use any other pie of your liking.)

Did you know . . . ?

 Paul McCartney named his 1997 solo album *Flaming Pie* in honor of something that John Lennon had once written about the origins of the Beatles: John's original use of the term *flaming pie* appeared in his 1961 *Mersey Beat* essay, "Being a Short Diversion on the Dubious Origins of The Beatles." In that essay, John wrote, "It came in a vision—a man appeared on a flaming pie and said unto them 'From this day on you are Beatles with an A.' Thank you, Mister Man, they said, thanking him."

A Beatles Magical Mystery Puzzle

ANSWER

1. I A**M** THE WALRUS
2. AND I LOVE H**E**R
3. **A**LL MY LOVING
4. TICKET **T**O RIDE

5. HELTER SKEL**T**ER
6. TELL ME W**H**Y
7. LOV**E** ME DO

8. BLACK**B**IRD
9. DEAR PRUDENC**E**
10. DRIVE MY C**A**R
11. I WAN**T** TO HOLD YOUR HAND
12. I WI**LL**
13. TH**E** END
14. **S**EXY SADIE

Solution:
MEAT THE BEATLES!

Index

About the Author

Stephen J. Spignesi specializes in popular-culture subjects, including television, film, contemporary fiction, and historical biography.

He has written several authorized entertainment books and has worked with Stephen King, Turner Entertainment, the Margaret Mitchell Estate, Andy Griffith, Viacom, and other entertainment industry personalities and entities on a wide range of projects. Mr. Spignesi has also contributed essays, chapters, articles, and introductions to many books.

Spignesi's books have been translated into several languages, and he has written for *Harper's, Cinefantastique, Saturday Review, Mystery Scene, Gauntlet,* and *Midnight Graffiti* magazines, as well as the *New York Times,* the *New York Daily News,* and the *New Haven Register.* Spignesi also appeared as a Kennedy family authority in the 1998 E! documentary, *The Kennedys: Power, Seduction, and Hollywood.*

In addition to writing, Mr. Spignesi lectures on a variety of popular-culture subjects and teaches writing in the Connecticut area. He is the founder and editor in chief of the small-press publishing company The Stephen John Press, which recently published the acclaimed feminist autobiography *Open Windows: The Autobiography of Charlotte Troutwine Braun.*

Spignesi is a graduate of the University of New Haven, and lives in New Haven with his wife, Pam, and their cat, Carter, named for their favorite character on *ER.*